The Secret of Change

Through Love And Forgiveness

Alen Božić

Books Boost Business

Who is the book for?

This book is written for people who grew up in all kinds of environments.

It is especially for younger people between the ages of 21 and 26 who are lost in life, or who suffer from depression or anxiety.

It is for those who are looking for answers and who want to know more about how life works.

The book is also intended for people who are wanting to make a change in their life and for people who feel that something more exists.

It is also for parents because they can see how to treat their children and what they as a parent can do for their child.

It is for everyone who suffers in life in any kind of way, as it is meant to make them realise that they are not the only ones and that there is hope for them, but they must want the change they must wish for it on their own.

Contents

"Imagine the world in which we inspire each other"

Alen Božić

Thank You Note

First of all, I would like to say thank you Creator and Spirit guides on all your guidance and support during this journey with the book and in my life.

Big thanks to my mother, Ljubica. She is still alive, and I am also thankful to my family who are not in this world anymore. Uncle Dinko Figać, my brother Nino Božić, my father Tihomir Božić, my grandmother Ankica Božić and my grandfather Josip Božić.

I would like to thank my wife Antonija and my son Leonardo. They were at my side for years and they lived through a lot of stress. Similarly, I would also like to thank Danijel Pavić, Ivan Jemrić and Igor Stanić for believing in me completely that I could write this book.

I would also like to thank my Theta Healing teacher, Goran Karna, for helping me learn the technique and for helping me heal myself. I am also incredibly grateful to the people who came into my life and who taught me and gave me lessons. I thank everyone who I have ever traumatised. Of course, I did not mean to. I am also thankful to you, the reader, for your trust and for reading this book.

Letter From The Author

Dear reader,

I would ask you in the very beginning before reading this book, that if you are planning on reading this book in the energy of judgement, please stop and let go of it.

This book is not for you.

Why?

In the book, I tell a lot of my "secrets" from my past. The intention of doing that is for them to be used as an example of what life can be like if you have that kind of mindset.

I was full of suffering, misery, resentment, anger, hatred and guilt, but I managed to get all these emotions out of my system, no matter which one, without a problem, and I managed to get into a state of bliss. Not just that. Today, I manage to love myself, which is one of the best accomplishments of a human being. The other reason is that judgement is just an energy of destruction, but not mine, yours. If you get to a point where you feel like judging, then you should know that you have something like that in your life, or you had it in this life or even a past life.

The same way, there is a chance you may get emotional when reading this book. You should know that this book is my personal truth and, in a way, it is a confession to the world. It does not matter if it is a confession or not, what matters is that it is the truth and my wish is to somehow touch the reader's heart and make you see that life can make sense, that everything can be solved, no matter how hard or dark your life is.

You should know that change is good and that it is welcome. It is up to you to decide which path you will take; you should know that there is an opportunity for everyone to change.

In the book, I talk a little bit about every major event in my life. It was not my intention to judge, nor did I go through the feeling of judgement towards anyone who was mentioned in the book. If I went through some sort of energy, it was healthy criticism, love, understanding, compassion and accepting of everything that is mentioned, including me.

If you are reading this, then it means that you have decided to read on. I wish that this book brings positive change to you in any way that is possible for you.

Enjoy reading.

"Do not judge another person, because you are judging yourself"

1.

Introduction.

I was born on the 2nd of August 1981 in Bjelovar, in Croatia. I grew up in Staro Štefanje. It is a small place between Bjelovar and Čazma.

At the time, I thought I had the best three years of my life. I will explain why later.

In December 1984, when I was three years old, well to be more precise four months after my third birthday, my brother Nino was born. It was at that moment that my world started to collapse, or so I thought.

My deepest, strongest memory I have from then is when my mother came back from the hospital with him. That memory cut so deep that I will never forget it. So basically, when I was three years old, I was obviously very young, and people came over, family and family friends. It felt like the spotlight was on Nino and my mother Ljubica, and that I was sitting in the shadow of them, unseen.

It is unbelievable how much it seemed to me that nobody noticed me. I remember all the compliments about how my brother was so cute and tiny, and me just standing there at the side and nobody saying things like that to me. I was not even acknowledged.

I was sad and I felt rejected by everyone around me. I wondered why it was like that, why didn't anyone ever notice me?

It was in those moments that I started hating and being jealous of my brother.

This all changed when I discovered Theta Healing.

It was this big trauma in my life from which everything started. As my brother grew up, of course I loved him, but on the other hand, I was also jealous at him for taking our mother's love. My mother loved him but seemed to forget about me. I was not forgotten in a material sense, but in a loving way, which was the most important thing I was concerned about.

As time passed, I became somewhat of a renegade in my family because of that lack of love (at least, that is what it felt like). I was a talented child with a high intelligence, which was confirmed by a lot of people, even in school.

In my school, there was a teacher called Ante Marković, who I started loving for the rest of my life.

He saw that I had talent and he supported me with school till 4th class. He even wanted to put me into 4th class from the 2nd class because he believed in me. I felt that from him, and I proved my talent to him every day.

I had the need to show off because I wanted my mother's love and attention.

My father was a little different from my mother as he "shared" his love equally towards my brother and me. He marked my childhood a little differently. In his soul, he was a good man, but he had a difficult life before me and my mother.

I will introduce you to my parents to whom I am grateful for bringing me into this world, and giving me this genetic make-up. I will explain why later. My mother was the child of an alcoholic and a grandma who I did not know much about, but I know that she left my mother and her brother in a foster home when she was four years old and went to Germany.

My mother did not experience a mother's love, and so she wasn't able to pass it on to me. She lived a life remarkably like mine, living in the shadow of the daughter of the parents who adopted her.

It was like the fairy tale, Ivek and Marica (in Croatian, this is Hanzel and Gretel), except this story was even sadder. How could she be happy when she grew up without a mother and without her love. When she was 17, she met my father, Tihomir. He was a mechanic at the time and was fixing a tractor of her adoptive parents.

I will now introduce you to my father in a few sentences as well. He was born in the house where I used to live, also in a household with an alcoholic father. My grandparents brought him into this world quite late because they were married for a while before he was born. My grandma was 29 when he was born back in 1956. My grandfather was born on the same date as my grandma, which was on the 27th of March 1927. My grandfather was an alcoholic and I do not know his reasons for being one, but my grandmother went through a lot with him. She had enough of him, and she found a lover; in fact, that lover is the reason for my father being born.

That is why I started the story with my grandparents so that I can explain the situation better. When my grandmother was pregnant, there were a lot of arguments about who the father was, and my father was in her womb at the time, and he was there through everything that happened. Through Theta Healing, we know that it is that way. It is interesting how a child's mind absorbs every emotion from its mother, believe me.

Later, I will tell you my story, where I witnessed a lot of different kinds of situations when I was in the womb.

Let us come back to my father. When he was born, he had a feeling of guilt for not belonging. He lived his entire life like that. Of course, at one point, it was subconscious guilt, which later manifested into reality. I have a feeling that my grandma intentionally scared my grandfather and told him that my father was not his son. It is interesting how much a human mind can create these kinds of situations just to feel powerful and to get some satisfaction from it. Later in life, my father even helped "his father" by working on his tractor, and he even earned money from it. So, he believed that he was someone else's son for the rest of his life. I believe that they did not talk about these things, but the truth was there, at least in his mind, and in the mind of a few other people from my village, if not all. He never told me his "secret", nor did he ever talk about it. I later found this out from my mother after he died at the age of 41. Somehow, I talked more about my father's life because his family is the reason for what I was before Theta Healing.

I will come back to primary school and proving that I was smart and that I meant something to my teacher. This came from the fact that even when I was five years old, my father gave me tasks to do, or to be exact, he put dots onto a piece of paper for me to connect to make letters. So, my father taught me how to write when I was five years old. Instead of me playing outside with my friends, I was preparing for school. This came from my father's wish for me to be successful and to head out on the path that he thought was the best for me to take. I accepted it all and I did everything that he wanted me to do, thinking that my mother would love me more and that I would be accepted and loved.

Everything was going great, and I thought I was receiving love and acceptance through all the compliments from my whole family, but all that fell apart when my brother turned five years old. I was in second class at the time. I was expecting my father to teach him how to write and do the same things he did with me, but guess what? He did not. In a way, I felt sorry about that. I even resented my father and mother about it, and even my brother too.

Through Theta Healing, I learnt that resenting is automatic when, in a deeper situation (trauma), we start resenting ourselves and others (family).

I am going to come back to the events that happened.

I noticed that nobody was doing anything about my brother. I waited until the moment when my brother would start to learn how to write. Sadly, that did not happen at the time. My brother was freely playing, while I was in school, giving everything I had to be as good as I could possibly be. I secretly hoped that my parents would tell him to start studying as well. I even tried to teach him, and I told them that it is not okay that I had to do it but that Nino did not. Their response was simply that he is different and that he is not particularly good at studying, as in let him play and enjoy himself while he is still little. Like, hellooo, where was I in this story?

What? Was I any different when I was his age? Thoughts like those flooded my head. I sometimes did stupid things to get attention, and I did get attention, but in a negative way, but it was attention and that was what I craved. Everyone scolded me and told me that I needed to be good, but I intentionally stayed the same because nobody understood me. Maybe I was rough with these words.

One person stands out in this story. That was my grandmother, Ankica. She was like a goddess in my life. Whenever I felt difficulties, she was there for me. Whenever I cried, was angry or got a bad grade, she was always there for me and supported me in everything. She complained if I did something wrong, but I felt her support and love in a positive way. What used to happen was that my grandma raised me, and what I became later was because of her raising me. We will get to that too. I am not saying that my parents did not raise me, but that they did not do it the right way. I never told you that I started wetting the bed after my brother was born, and this happened quite often, and I was even ashamed of it and I hid it in school. Nobody knew about it. If you are reading this book, some friends from school would be incredibly surprised.

In school, I acted tough and I never gave in on myself. Maybe I stood out in class in a bad way, but I never gave in. I even acted rough sometimes. Now, imagine a tough child who wets his bed. That is why I hid that secret very well. I even hid it from my parents, when I could. My mother took me to a psychiatrist because of it, and the answer was simple: jealousy towards my brother. See, even now, something physically manifested and I was guilty again for what I was doing. My parents never saw that they were the ones in the wrong, but they saw me doing wrong things. At least, that is what it seemed like to me.

As far as I can remember, my mother used to buy me toys and I feel like she wanted to show me that she loved me that way. On the other hand, my brother got toys as well, but he got something else as well, something that cannot be bought, and that is love. That beautiful word. It's so beautiful, but what is more beautiful is feeling it from someone else. Love between people should be unconditional, which means we give it and expect nothing in return. A lot of people today love, but they have conditions for that love. When we impose conditions on love and if something does not happen the way it is supposed to, we get hurt, and we feel guilt and even resentment.

For the world to look good, people need to love unconditionally. You may be wondering, well how is it possible to love that way? Well it is possible to love your children and all the people that way. I will talk about this later when we get to the wonderful moment when I regained unconditional love back into my life. I am now getting memories of my grandmother. You could say that she was the only person in my life from whom I felt this beautiful unconditional love. My mother gave me love by buying me toys, but there are no good memories of the unconditional love like I got from my grandmother. To me, that feeling is especially important, it is not just a feeling, it is everything that there is. The entire creation is based on that feeling and it would all disappear if there were no love. That is how my childhood "disappeared" when I rejected unconditional love and when I did not believe in it. I was five years old, and I was minding my brother. I do not even remember properly, but I know one thing, I was minding him and he broke a plate. When my parents saw what had happened, they both abused me and beat me, and the memory of my father's anger was carved into my memory at that moment. My mother also hit me a few times, but my father beat me completely. That is when I stopped believing that unconditional love exists. I was innocent and I still got in trouble, but my brother obviously did not. He was younger; therefore, I was the one who was supposed to make sure that everything was okay. It was a big responsibility for a five-year-old.

I am not writing this in self-pity. I am writing this to show you that these things can affect you, but that they can be changed later in life. If you believe in yourself and in your life, know that there is a way to help yourself, your family and your friends. Believe me, I am writing this with tears in my eyes – not sad tears, but, yes, joyful tears. I just know that these words will bring you hope and wishes for a better life. As I am writing this, I am writing it with unconditional love, and it's exciting to imagine the change in you and your success in every aspect. Success is possible, no matter what. I feel like everyone who reads this book will feel that. I can guarantee it. If you believe in yourself and in what you do, no matter what anyone else says, I can guarantee you will be successful.

2.

My Story

Let us continue with my story because this was only the beginning. Nothing was the same after that. I rejected what kept us moving, but not completely – I just pushed it away deep inside of me. I just did not believe that it was possible that I had to get hurt, even though I was completely innocent, by the people who were expected to love me that way. Unfortunately, I gave up on getting unconditional love. Now, I am thankful to my parents because of it. I know that sounds weird. How can someone be thankful to someone for not being loving and thankful for being abused? That was the best thing, as they were a good example of what not to be, even though I found it hard to cross the subconscious programmes. To be exact, I was failing.

Before I found out about Theta Healing, this was the start to my spiritual awakening, I mean spiritually, materially and physically. Later through life, I was getting worse. I was breaking the rules in different ways. I was causing trouble. I was a "rebel", and I was not sorry. Not only were my parents "against" me, so were others and they all criticised me, saying that I was mean and I should act nicely. I only laughed at those critics and stayed completely the same, and sometimes behaved worse.

I remember one situation where there was a big trauma. I was with my other grandmother's husband. My grandmother was divorced, and she lived with him. His name was Sakib. My brother, my uncle Dinko and I went into a café, and we all sat at one table. They told me that I was worthless and told me to go sit at another table. They ordered drinks for each other but not for me. You can imagine what I felt like at that time. I wanted to just disappear from this world. I was innocent at the time and there were no reasons for them to treat me that way. They told me I was bad and that I did not deserve their company. I again blamed my brother for this because he was the one who everyone liked. At least, that is what I saw.

Later, I got another low blow from Sakib. He had a polaroid camera and, at the time, it was a miracle to be able to take a picture and have it come out straight away. Well, they wanted a photo together without me. Everyone who was supposed to be in the photo were Sakib, my Aunt Ervina, my Aunt Edina and my brother. What about me??? Where was I in that story? Of course, I was shocked and saddened, and I started crying. Then, they told me to come and take a picture with them. I felt terrible, I felt discarded. It was as if I did not deserve good things in life. My own family were pushing me aside, as if they did not want me. That was when I was made to believe that I was worthless, that I did not deserve anything in life. How could I deserve anything when everyone disregarded me?

It was not normal for it to be like that. Well, that is what I thought back then.

They were the painful experiences that brought me the strength that pushed me forwards. I wanted to prove to others that I meant something, that I did deserve to be treated properly and that I deserved everything in life. Now, I know that it is not like that, but that was the most crystal-clear thing in my mind at the time.

Let us continue. I think that with these memories, I have acquired enough energy. As you can see, everything comes down to me living in my brother's shadow. Nothing drastic happened when I was six years old. That is when I got my first bike. It was a BMX, which was a big deal at the time. To have a bike like that was an honour, but guess what? My father bought the bike early and I had to look at the bike instead of ride it. It was sad to have something like that and not use it. It was mean. They said I was too little and that I did not have any understanding of it. Why did they buy it in the first place then? It was as if I was some animal, keeping me from something that meant a lot to me, letting me look at it but not giving it to me. Even animals do not deserve that. I know this sounds ungrateful, but in a child's mind, there is no space for understanding everything. A child does not understand a lot, like parents and grown-ups do. Those are the kind of things that a lot of people do not understand, and they raise their children not understanding that.

Now, I am thankful for everything, but back then I felt horrible. So, the day when I was supposed to get my bike came. It was a Sunday. I remember it as if it were yesterday. My mother brought the bike out of a room where it was stored and had collected dust. It was an amazing experience to sit down on my BMX and to push the pedals. I was so proud of myself, and happy and grateful to my mother and father for letting me finally use my bike. I headed uphill through my little village and I was so happy with that experience.

When I was going back, I was going quite fast. There were works being done on a nearby house and there was a tractor parked by my house, and I was going downhill extremely fast. In front of the house, there was a barrel and some sand. As I was going down, I used my intelligence. I knew exactly how to manoeuvre around it to not get hit or hit something. I remember that there was a 1.5-metre gap in between the tractor and the barrel, and I knew that I could fit right in between and not hit anything. My mother witnessed all this happening because she was sitting on a bench under a cherry tree just outside the house.

Nothing was hit, no one was hurt, there was not a scratch on the bike. What do you think happened?

I did not have my bike after that, not because I crashed it, but because my mother took it away from me. So, it was my first cycle ride, my first time on a bike, and I was riding it for about ten minutes, and I lost it. I was waiting for it for so long, seeing it gathering dust. I was so sad and in tears too. I was begging my mother not to put it away, but she did not see me, she did not see my emotions. She just saw herself and how much she wanted to punish me, and nothing else. It is sad, but that is how I lived through that moment. I was also beaten. As if it were not enough that I had my bike taken away, I was hit too! It was honestly one of the worst moments of my childhood. I felt soft, weak, deflated and unloved. Everything that I did not want to happen was happening to me. Nothing ever went the way I wanted it to go. I cried for so long that day that I had a such a bad headache. I cried until I had no tears left to cry. The worse thing was that my mother blamed me for it all, but I knew that I could fit through the gap. She saw the whole situation and that I did not crash. She had her own point of view and did not want to let it go. She just wanted to punish me. Half a year passed before I got my bike back and I was so happy when I did. This time nothing happened to me for them to take it away from me. Did my parents figure out that they were too strict? I doubt it.

I do not want to talk about all the negative things that happened to me, so I will start mentioning about the good experiences. Of course, there were good experiences, but somehow the negative ones really cut into my subconscious. When this happens, they later take control.

At the time, there were some good things happening. I remember going to the Zoo in Zagreb. I was little, but after going to the Zoo, a lot of good things started happening to me. I remember the lions, the snakes, the monkeys and many other animals. There were a lot of jokes passed around and, overall, it was a good time with my parents and my brother. I will never forget when instead of saying camel (grbadeva), I said Grandma Eva (baba Eva), which my parents found so funny that later they told a lot of people about it. I felt pleasure as people finally started noticing me even though they were laughing at me. Ha ha, I was acknowledged for what was going through my head. When I looked back on it, I perceived things the other way and I started realising that people were in fact making fun of me and laughing at me, but at the time, I did not notice it, I just accepted that it was something normal. Well, it is not normal for someone to make fun of you and for you to feel loved because of it. The human mind is interesting because it can so easily fool us to the point where we cannot even notice it. Anyway, I was pleased with myself and that is what mattered to me. That was also the first time I had seen exotic animals, which was a wonderful experience.

It was an amazing experience going back to school because I was very experienced. Remember, how I told you that my father had taught me how to spell and write? Yes, I know it is contradicting. First, I complained about how my father made me write, and now I am saying how I could not wait to go into school to prove myself. That is the point. School gave me the opportunity to show off and to prove myself to others. I knew I could do this because I considered myself intelligent. I was thankful to my father for that. It was important for me to go to school to prove myself, but not to study anything. I hope that this experience helps people who are now parents and, of course, those who are going to be parents one day.

Let's go to the story where we were going to the seaside on a holiday after I finished school that year. Ah, that's the life. While my mother and father argued about how they were going to finance the holiday, my brother and I were so excited about it. After all, it was a new experience. I was seven years old at the time and my brother was four years old. They finally decided to go; after all, we had free accommodation there. My father's friend invited us to come to his holiday home. The house was on the island of Krk in a place called Punat, of course, in Croatia. My parents barely had enough money for a holiday in Croatia, so they did not even think about going abroad. That is not important right now, what was important was that we all made it there. Aaah, what a beautiful day. The first meeting with the sea and swimming with my parents, who behaved like completely different people than usual. They were completely different, there was no arguing, no anger, no yelling. Yaaaaay, that is what was so good. If only every day was like that, I could stay there for the rest of my life. At the seaside, there are not any problems. At least, that is what I thought for four whole days.

Then yes, something bad happened. That day, we were supposed to have a barbeque. Everything was going great and everyone was happy, when suddenly, my father started shaking, like a branch in the wind. It was a stroke. Who could imagine, when everything was good, everyone was loving each other, there was joy all around, that boom, something like that could happen? I could not believe that it was happening. Seeing my father in that situation was not easy. Even though he was bad sometimes, I still loved him. He was my dad. As children, we had to stay in the holiday home while our parents went to the hospital to get help. It was not drastic, but it was still a trauma. I remember that, back then, I'd memorised a popular song that went "Here's life and everything, I am giving you my prayers" and I sung "Fu*k life and everything, how is this possible". So, as a child, I started to hate life and I believed that when it's the best time of your life, that's when something bad happens. Now, I know that this was a subconscious programme from my ancestors, like my father and, of course, like me.

I will tell you later about my programming. Eventually, the vibrant energy completely disappeared there. My mother was scared and worried for my father, and my brother and I were not enjoying anything in the same way afterwards, worrying about our dad. My father recovered from the stroke and we went home. That was some holiday. It was supposed to be an excellent experience and a great memory, but it ended up being the complete opposite. The worse thing from all of it is that was the beginning of my father's strokes and heart attacks. I will explain about that in a different part of the book, when I start talking about Theta Healing. I will talk more about positive things and, in the end, everything will be positive. Even now, I am writing this with a positive attitude and with a big change, which is interesting because I am writing this from my soul, and I love what I am doing.

Let us continue.

Eventually school started and I started to forget what happened during the holiday. Thanks to school, my childhood went along smoothly. While my parents and I were supposed to be doing something, I used the excuse that I had to study. This meant that my parents had great expectations of me, but when my brother came up, they just said that he is not for school. There was one situation where I did not get away with working out in the fields. Well, it was a bad day, an unbelievably bad day. I was pulling potatoes out of the ground and since I had just started school, I obviously had no schoolwork to do. Everyone started telling me to go out and work because you must work in life. "You will not have anything in life if you don't work" everyone around me said. I do not know what happened to everyone around me, but it felt like the entire world was turning on me. How could I not feel like this, when everyone kept telling me to work and started attacking me verbally. It was hard. What had happened to everyone? Why did they suddenly start attacking me? First, they would say something and then they would change their minds. They were contradicting themselves. If I was made for school, then I was made for school, not for heavy physical work. I agreed to go with them, but the entire day was bad, and my brother saw me and all he did was have fun without a care in the world. I am telling you that I was confused. I did not know why everyone was like that, there was no explanation. Why would someone who is successful at school have to work hard for a living. Back then, I did not know how to ask why they were acting that way, because those were the kinds of things that happen automatically. It just cuts into your subconscious. That part that I remember about working on the fields was horrid. Sometime later, there was a corn harvest, and nearly the same situation happened again. I could not believe that this was happening to me, with everyone constantly attacking me. I was a child then, and children are not like adults. Children cannot understand things like that. That day passed and it all went back to normal. School, studying, but studying did not interest me much anymore. Why should I study if I must work? I studied, but not with the same passion as before. It was as if something was holding me back. I did not know what it was because I was not aware, and I did not know how things worked. By that, I mean that I think in a way that I knew I could do it and that I knew my full potential.

It is also another reason why I am writing this book – to make you aware of what a person can go through in their life and that they can still rise above it. To rise above means to understand that it does not mean that others are below you, but to realise that we are a part of God and that we are not separated in any way. Every day, I appreciate these things and I enjoy them. I enjoy looking at how this creation works. I am amazed by it and I am thankful that the Creator created this reality as it is. That is not all. He gave us the ability to create our own reality and free will too. Wow, that is the truth, that is why I said that I was not aware of myself in the past. Up until now, I have talked about things that were deeply cut into my subconscious.

From seven or eight years old, nothing exciting happened. The same things just kept happening time and time again. That was the last year that I was at the seaside together with my parents. Everything rotated around that, and the fact that they loved me and my brother unconditionally. My father was a realist, but he was sometimes very bad towards us. My grandfather loved my brother, but nobody cared about me. I never got praise from my grandfather or my mother. She of course loved my brother, but she constantly ignored me, showing no love. I am not saying she did not love me. I am saying that she always expressed her love for me with toys and other material things. I did not want toys. I wanted hugs and kisses. I wanted her love. I wanted the love from the person who gave birth to me, the person who created me and put me in this world. It is amazing how the Creator cared for me and gave me a grandmother who loved me with all her heart, and in some ways, I considered her my mother, which you will see further on in the book.

I wanted to write this book in chronological order, but my soul has decided differently.

There was one event that I remember from my childhood, when I was six years old. It was a Sunday, and the neighbours were sitting on a bench in the shade. I was a nuisance as a child, and my mother would tell me to stop doing all kinds of things, but I would just keep doing them. She did not have any patience for that. Usually, she was in fear and in low vibrations. When she got angry at me, she would tie me to a fence outside of our house and tell me that now I can demonstrate how I can be calm. That was humiliating. My mother tied me up like an animal and I sat with the neighbours watching me. I cannot describe how hard it was for me. I cried and I tried to cut the rope to be free, but with no success. I was defeated, humiliated, shamed and rejected, all in that instance. It was terrible. She let me go after an hour. It was such a difficult experience, and I stayed ashamed and humiliated after that. That was not all.

After a few days, a similar situation happened, where I was playing, and I remember I tipped something over and broke it. My mother went crazy, and she put me into a room where there was no light, it was completely dark. It was a massive trauma. During my childhood, they scared me with the dark, saying that monsters and witches were in the dark. I ended up in that room where there was no light at all, just the dim light coming from under the door. I cannot describe with words the feelings I felt. I desperately kept banging the door in the hope of being let out. I was in tears, with a raw voice from fear. I was shaking uncontrollably. I still shudder when I remember those moments. I am not saying that I did not deserve punishment; however, this was extreme. My mother said that she did not know what to do with me, that she had to do something that would teach me to calm down.

Oh mother, not like that, any other kind of punishment could have taught me a lesson. When a child is born, it is raised with love, you treat it with love, happiness, joy, and you enjoy the child's company. You show it that it is loved, and if something bad happens, you need to explain to the child why it should not do that and to warn it – with words, not fists – so that what happened does not happen again. A lot of parents tend to just punish or hit a child without an explanation. That was how I was raised, by my mother and father. I was a reflection of how they raised me. I learnt lessons from those punishments and, if I had not, I would not be writing this.

Sometimes, I wrote down what was different and what was not. Maybe, in reality, I was not even that bad, but I was constantly being told that I was. I personally think that a child cannot be bad. A child reflects their parents. So, in my family, there was something wrong. I am not blaming them for anything, but I am just thinking realistically. The time I was tied to the fence was not the only time when that happened. A year and a half later, my parents were building another room onto the house, and in that room, there were supports which were supporting the ceiling whilst we were waiting for the concrete to dry. My brother and I were playing, and we played a kind of prank. Our father went crazy and tied us up together to those supports. Somehow, it was a lighter punishment from him. He still punished us together, it was not just me who got punished. What would have happened if my mother had punished us? He told us to stay tied up for two hours to learn how to behave. It was a fair punishment, I must admit. Tie children like slaves. It was a trauma too, but somehow it was easier for me because my brother was with me, so the punishment was evenly distributed between us, for once. If only it stayed that way, but I was braver than my brother and I started whining and complaining about the punishment and, of course, our parents heard me. Yes, I paid for the fact that I was not satisfied, and I paid a lot. After a while, our father came and I do not remember if two hours had passed or not, as I did not have a watch. He untied my brother because he was calm and obedient, and of course I had to stay tied up. Then it hit me. How can he do that to me? Am I really such a nothing and a nobody that he can treat me like that? That is when I started crying so hard that my head started to hurt. That feeling of defeat, rejection and misunderstanding overwhelmed me. I even wished that I were no longer alive. "What did I do to deserve this life?" and "Why is this happening to me?", I thought to myself. Unfortunately, I already hated my mother and father for everything. I did not just hate them, I was also disgusted by them, by me, by my brother, by God, by life.

It was the same story throughout most of my life. I simply saw myself as the victim, but not the victim who begs for attention, but the victim who is brave, strong and knows that he can handle everything. There were suicidal thoughts going through my mind, but I overcame them with the thought of a better tomorrow. Somehow, I always had that in a part of my mind. Everything is going to be great when I grow up.

Now everything is great. I'm big and I feel grown-up, but on the inside. That is what is important – for a human to feel powerful, strong, joyful, to love life, to love the people around them, to love the Mother Earth and, of course, to love God. Later, I will explain how I got these positive thoughts which led me to my current life and, of course, my future life.

Then, the lower vibrations would overwhelm me, but now, the higher ones are here. They are so high that I love life, I am happy, and I love and accept people. I do not argue with anyone. I may sometimes exchange a few words with my wife, but there are no heavy emotions and I quickly get over them. In the other part of the book, I will talk a lot more about these beautiful vibrations that a lot of people today remove from their lives and do not want to admit that they have.

Not a lot of time had passed before another disaster happened. It was my father. I came home from school one day and I saw that everyone in the house was sad. Everyone's heads were down. I asked them what happened. My grandmother said: "Your mother is in the hospital. Your father was taken ill, and they went to the hospital." Even though he abused me, I still loved him and, at the time, I was not even thinking about the times he abused me. Instead, I thought about him and I started wondering whether he was alive and what I would do if he did die. I was as shocked by the news as my family was. I went into the living room, where I was crying and thinking all by myself. "Is everything I've been through not enough?" I asked God. "Do you have to take my father too? What did I do to deserve to be punished all the time?"

These were common questions I asked in my life, for which I might have got answers, but I did not know how to recognise them. I had that mindset that God punishes. That is because I was raised in a Christian family and I am Catholic now. I believe in God, Jesus and a lot of things that we learn in the Catholic religion. Then, I had a different mindset about these things. I believed that God punished us, but it is not like that. Everything that happens, happens because the soul wants to experience it, and not because God wants to punish us. In a way, God wants that because he gave us free will and he loves us unconditionally, and what we want he gives us unconditionally. I will tell you something I told some older Catholic lady once, because she had old beliefs in God. I told her this:

"When a human does something wrong, the reason is the devil, but when something happens that wasn't according to a plan, it's God's fault because he had to punish you, but when a human does something right and is proud of it, he is the reason for that."

Isn't it interesting, now you know what I am talking about? A lot of you can certainly recognise yourself in this. We are 100% responsible for our life and it's nobody's fault, not even ours, because it is wrong to carry the guilt that you get when you do something "bad" in life.

Back to my father. My mother came home later from the hospital and she said that my father had had a stroke and that he could not move his left arm. He could barely lift it up, and it was awfully bad. It was difficult seeing my mother in a state like that. My brother was still small, so he did not understand what was happening. He cried because he saw us crying. My grandmother was also sad, and she told me that she believed that I would be something and a someone one day. Those words really made me feel better, and they meant a lot to me. Someone did believe in me after all, no matter what my behaviour. My grandfather was just quiet, and it seemed as if he did not love us or my father. That is what I thought at the time.

Now, I would say that he did not know any different than to quietly endure his pain and sadness. The next day, we went to visit my father at the Bjelovar hospital. It was a hard day. We came to him and he greeted us in tears, and he was hugging me and my brother. Somehow, he was hugging me more, maybe because I am older and I would have to take care of the family if he passed away. That is when he told us that he nearly died that night and that he thought he would not make it through the night. That is why he wrote his will. Imagine this, he thought of me. It was unbelievable that, after all the torture, he still fully believed in me, even though sometimes he did not show it in a way that I could understand it. If he only told me openly everything he thought. In the will, he wrote that I should get the car, that was the only thing he owned. I was pleasantly shocked. Wow, if my dad dies, I get a car, I thought to myself. I know it sounds bad, but it's honest. That was just my thought process, which happens to people quite often. To me it happened, but subconsciously. I really wanted to have my own car. Even though I was little, around eight years old, I think that it is a dream of every male child to have a car, and I just got the opportunity to become an owner of my first car. The visit to my father ended and I left the hospital quite happy. If something happens, I will get to keep the car. I will not be without anything, I will have the car, I thought. Later, in the story, there was some resistance from my mother. She told me that I would not get the car, that I was too little to own something like that and that she would do whatever she wanted with the car.

Finally, things started going well in my life. I nearly got a car, but then my mother got involved and wanted that for herself. "You cannot do this to me, who are you to take what I got?" I thought to myself. Somehow, I thought I was going to get that car because everyone was saying that my father would not get well soon, and I understood that as he was going to die soon. This is going to sound bad, but I could not wait for that day to come. You need to know that, at that age, I did not understand at the time what someone dying meant. I was just focused on my dream, the dream that one day I would have my own car. That was important to me at the time. My car. And, yet again, nothing.

My father got better and was much better than before. I do not know if I was hurt because of that. I knew that if something like this happened again, I would get what I wanted. I did not want something bad to happen, but I also did not wish it. I just believed that my father would give me the car one day. My father was not the problem at the time, it was my mother who would have taken from me what I'd earned. I was not in the slightest enthusiastic about her attitude and I did not have any understanding about it. At the time of the recovery of my father, my family decided to sell a house in a place called Žabno. It was the inheritance from my grandmother. We wanted to upgrade our house and put a new roof on it. There was enough money to build an entire house and mostly finish it. Before the works began, my father began going to rehabilitation in the nearby springs. I do not know how, but the money was with my mother and not with my grandmother. We often came to visit my father and we lived informally at that time. I remember the excitement I had about trying out hamburgers and the smell of French fries. My mother was not spending money in vain. I think she had some money put by, but I do not think it was a lot. It was my grandmother who felt bad about us spending all her inherited money, instead of using the money to work on the house. Every day, she complained about us spending the money. I was on her side, as she was the one who loved me, protected me and took good care of me. That is why I believed that my mother was spending everything and not saving anything for the house. Eventually, the works on the house finally started. I was happy, as at least something grand was happening in my life. Now, I will have my own room and my brother will have his own room. That was the plan. Alen will get a new storey and can live there. At the time, I did not even have my own room and now I was supposed to have an entire storey for myself. I could not wait for that to be built and to say that I have something material that I can say that I own. At that time, a war had started.

So, between selling the house in the other village and upgrading the house, eighteen months had passed. We were waiting for my father to get well so he could get the materials. It was interesting watching the builders build the house and creating my area. I remember one day that the roof was mostly done and an air raid siren went off. The builders were putting tiles on the roof. There was lots of banter. They were covering the house in case the planes came and dropped bombs, and destroyed all their work in a second. It was just some banter, but you never knew.

My parents had decided to start working on the house at the right time. They said at the time that the war would never come close to us and that we were in an area where the war would not come. I believed them, and somehow, I knew it was like that. The house was done, but the finish was rough. And again, I was left hanging. They said that I would get my own storey and, in the end, it was just naked walls and nothing more. I was disappointed again. How could they do that? They promised something and then they did not go through with it. They said it was because we did not have enough money. That is when I remembered the story with my grandmother. My mother had spent most of the money and that was why the house was not completely finished. That is when I realised that we had enough money to build an entire house from the ground up, but they'd only built a single, unfinished storey. I often talked with my grandma about this, and we talked about things behind my mother's back. I was sad because I did not have anything. Well, I had something, but I could not enjoy it. The worst thing of all is that they did not make a bathroom and a toilet. That was a wish I had my entire childhood. A bathroom and a toilet, inside. I resented my parents for so long. I was even ashamed that I did not have anywhere to shower or to go to the toilet. Most of the people in the village had that, but we did not. Now, we had money and still we did not make anything we should have made. Honestly, if they just used all the money just for a bathroom and toilet, I would have been so happy. I would have had somewhere to shower decently, and I could have gone to the toilet properly. We usually went to the toilet in the outhouse.

When I remembered that, I immediately felt sick. It was probably because I really wanted a proper toilet. My parents were "zatrajanci" (Croatian slang for people who are wasting money on nothing) as my grandmother used to say, and I thought that too, until I started to do Theta Healing. They were not "zatrajanci", but they had those kinds of subconscious programmes which are a lot stronger for us than on a conscious level. No matter what, a part of me was pleased with the house, because at least it was not small anymore. Now, it was big and there was hope that it was going to get finished one day. Somehow, deep inside of me, I wanted to have the same things as the rich people in my village. I did not think of having the exact same things, I just wanted abundance in my life. By abundance, I mean to be affluent, have a nice house that has been done up inside and out, a nice yard, a nice car... But I did not have any of those things in my childhood and it looked as if my parents were not going to have anything that I considered to be of great value. I felt sorry about that. I again blamed myself, God and everything around me, because I did not have anything. Nobody ever told me that everything is of value, and I mean everything, but only if you see it that way. If you watched my life before Theta Healing, I had limited assets and, in my childhood, it was the same, just in a different way. It looked to me like I had an abundance of problems, abuse, misunderstanding. The only good abundance I remember was my grandmother's unconditional love. Everything else was "bad" abundance. We conclude that abundance is everything around us, but what kind of abundance we have in our life depends mostly on us, and we should put responsibility on ourselves for every event in our life.

I said responsibility, not guilt. Today, people often mix the two emotions. Somehow, they all say "I am guilty" or "They are guilty", but really nobody is guilty of anything and, on the other hand, we are all responsible, but not for others, for ourselves. We are responsible for accepting ourselves and loving others no matter what mistakes they make.

Everything happens for a reason and if we look at things that way, it is much easier for us to live. The ease of living in abundance is possible for everyone and it's available no matter what age you are or what gender you are.

Let us go back to the time when there was a war in "our beautiful" (Croatia). I thought back then that it all started because of a football game called Dinamo-Red Star. There was an argument between the players and there was chaos at the stadium. I watched the game with my family, and I absorbed their emotions, which were opposing moods. Hate was flowing in from all sides, and I considered something like that normal because I lived with them. That is when I had a different view of the people of Serbia, because I was influenced by my family. To tell you straight away, it is not like that anymore. I remember my father grinding his teeth from all the hate and he wished he were on that stadium to support his "Bad Blue Boys". Somehow, as a child, I really wanted to be like my father. He was a big influence on me. In the family, we all learn how to be a man from our father figures and we learn how to treat our significant others from our mothers. The role models in the family we belong to build our personality and how we react with others, and what paths we follow. Later, our whole life seems to be mapped out, but we are just not aware of it.

My father was saying that it is over now, that there will undoubtedly be a war. I remember the poor, naïve people who were squirted with water by the police. The game was at the stadium in Zagreb. Even though they were on local ground, the fans of Dinamo were sprayed with water from fire trucks and were beaten by the police. I know that I felt the excitement and support from my father, and I wanted to be there with my him.

Why are they fighting our people when they have not done anything? This was some heavy injustice. At least, that is how I saw it back then. I was so proud at the time of Zvonimir Boban, who while running, hit a policeman who was beating a fan with a baton. It was an exciting experience at the time and, yet again, it gave me another chance to get closer to my father. I thought that if I was like him that I would be accepted by him. However, I was accepted in a way, but not as much as I wanted to be. Oh yes, those expectations. Whenever I anticipated something, it did not go the way I thought it should have gone. At the time, I did not know the answer, but today it's clear why it went like that. Expectations create disappointments in life. If you live your life without expectations, you will live a more peaceful and happier life.

As bad as the war sounded, and I know a lot of people were hurt and suffered from it, I considered it an interesting period of my life. My uncle went to war and often came back to see us. I was proud of the fact that he was my uncle and that he was brave for fighting. My uncle was very disgusting towards me and he did not love me much, but of course he loved my brother. He loved me too I suppose, but in a weird way. Sometimes I was good for him, then sometimes I was not. There were a lot of situations where I disappointed him, so I carried the guilt that I had disappointed him. One time, he was so drunk that he broke the door and he just put a sticker where he broke it. He lived in a house that was owned by my grandmother Katica. He was put there and did not live in his own house. My grandmother was strict and scrappy. In confidence, one day, I told my younger aunt about the door, thinking she would keep my secret. I wanted to get closer to my aunt so that our relationship could be much better than it was. Now, imagine this, I told her that and around an hour later after my aunt left, we were going to see my grandmother because she lived just beside our house. My uncle's behaviour was weird, and he looked at me weirdly, and of course I realised that he knew what I'd told my aunt. I was so afraid then. I feared my uncle, as he was a little bit crazy and he often did stupid things like getting into fights and stealing, all bad things. That is the way he grew up, without parents to correct him, so he did not know any different.

Now, imagine failing someone like that. It was not so easy for me and a lot of things passed through my head. Later, he got his chance. He started shouting at me. He was screaming that he would rip my head off, and that I was a traitor and that he hated me. I cannot even repeat all the terrible things he said to me. If my mother were not there, I think I would have filled my pants. I told him I was sorry and that it would not happen again, but that did not please him. He told me that he would not tell me anything like that again. He said that he did not trust me anymore. I was disappointed in myself for my actions. I resented myself, I hated myself, but of course I did not resent him. This experience was cut into my brain. Later, I always had that feeling that I had let him down. Whenever he looked at me the wrong way, I had that feeling every time. No matter what though, I was still proud of my uncle when he went to war. When he came back from the battlefields, the pride came back to me, and I would boast that he was my uncle. Not everyone is brave enough to go to the front lines and fight.

Today, I see that that is not bravery, but madness. Back then, it was the way I wrote it down. It was when I had my first encounter with a weapon. It was remarkably interesting. When the soldiers came back, they had a van full of ammo, guns, grenades and rockets. As a child of ten years of age, I was fascinated by them. I used to get plastic guns as toys, but now I had a chance to see various weapons in real life. I even started to collect bullets and various things my uncle took from the war. He brought mine shrapnel and the fins from rockets. I enjoyed seeing them. Back then, the world spun around weapons. It was mostly like that.

My imagination was doing its work and I did not know any different. My brother also participated in collecting with me. Even with everything that was going on, we loved each other. He even loved me more than I did him. I was jealous that he was cuddly and that everyone loved him, yet he loved me unconditionally. I know that I said only my grandmother loved me, but here is another reason why I am writing this book. To show you what it means to consciously write what I am going to write in another part. That just happened to me.

I was becoming aware that my brother loved me unconditionally while I was writing this book for you.

There is an answer to the saying "If you give, you will be given". The Christmas holidays of 1991 came, and we celebrated at my grandmother's. It was interesting, the entire family was gathered together and it was pure banter. I felt great to be surrounded by the entire family. I even felt accepted. You can imagine the shock. I could not believe it. My father was suddenly starting to breathe heavily and he was rolling his eyes. My mother took him out to get some fresh air and she put a tablet for his heart under his tongue. He usually carried tablets with him because he'd had heart problems before. So back then, my father was 35 years old, and he was having heart problems. A similar situation happened when we were at the seaside. It is unbelievable how whenever it would get nice for me and I started enjoying something, a lot of bad things started happening. This was constantly in my thoughts. In the end, as my dad did not feel any better, we had to go home. It was the end of the celebrations again. It was all ruined by one thing – my father.

I felt sorry for my father, but at the same time, I was asking myself why this was happening to me. What is going on? What did I do to God to deserve this? The next day, my father felt better, thank God for that. We used to enjoy company, so the next day we continued celebrating the holidays. It was like that every day and, for us kids, this was something special. New Year's Eve came by and something unexplainably amazing happened. My uncle was drinking, he was very intoxicated. We came to my grandmother's house where we were going to celebrate New Year's.

Because my uncle was in the war, he had a lot of weapons. Of course, he began shooting with his gun occasionally. Later that night, when he had used all the ammo that he had at home, he went to a neighbour where he had an entire bag full of ammo and bombs. My grandmother and the older people were trying to calm him down and were trying to prevent him from doing anything stupid, but he did not listen to them. That is when he threw seven grenades in the yard and shot around 500-1,000 bullets with his gun. For us children, it was interesting, exciting, thrilling, but the older people were scared in case anything bad happened, but they were also scared of standing up to my uncle to make him stop. My uncle gave me and my brother a chance to shoot the gun. He was holding the gun, while we pulled the trigger. It was an amazing experience.

Unfortunately, my uncle ended up in custody the next day. Someone reported him to the police. I judged those people at the time, because they betrayed my uncle, but then I remembered that I had done the same. I was no longer the traitor, but I was the one to judge. I thought that it was the right choice. On the other hand, I wanted to be like my uncle, and for others to fear me and to be bold like him. In my world at the time, it was logical that everyone who was strong and powerful was "bad" and did stupid things. I liked that formula and I started to develop it, and I thought that, in that way, I too would be strong and powerful.

Later in life, I realised that it is not like that, but then as a child, I believed in that kind of power and strength. It is always easier to incline towards bad behaviour than to do good. At least, I thought so at the time.

So, 1992 came by and that was the year that kind of twisted my life to be graver. At the start of the year, my dad had a terrible heart attack just after the Christmas holidays. He was in hospital for quite some time. Believe me, I do not even remember anything about what happened, but I was shocked for I do not even know how long. He still had not recovered from the stroke; he could barely move his left arm.

He was recovering all year. Now, I am having visions of my mother crying. She was so scared, for herself, for my father and for us. My brother and I were already used to this, but we were still sad because of our father. My grandmother was crushed, and my grandfather was always silent in his thoughts. You could see that he was worried or that he was sorry. He acted so emotionless. I even judged him for it. How can he be like that? His child was nearly dying, and he was being so cold-hearted. It took a lot of time for my father to recover and, as far as I remember, my life was school and hospital. The regular absence of my mother when she went to visit my father ended up meaning that we were more in the hospital than at home. When he came back from the hospital, everyone was around him except my grandfather. He did not try too much. I was not pleased with that, but I still judged his behaviour. I felt sorry for my father and his state. He was very decrepit from shock and the potions that he'd received in the hospital. I wanted him to get better so that our relationship in the family could become good again and so that things would start heading in a positive way.

A few months passed and he was feeling better. He still needed to go to therapy, but his health was much better. He was moving his left arm with some difficulty, which was a side effect of the stroke, but overall, he was well. The only bad thing was that he started to gain weight, which was not good for him or his heart. It is as if he was being self-destructive and wanted another heart attack or stroke. The truth is that subconsciously he really thought like that, which is unbelievable, but it is true. Unfortunately, that is how it works, if you are healthy and are of average weight, diseases would not reoccur much worse. But it was not his consciousness that wanted that to happen, it was his subconscious that liked everyone around him helping him and giving him love. My father did not know that love can be given and received in health, which today, thank God, I know and use.

The entire story is about love. It is particularly important to first love yourself and accept yourself completely. When we accept ourselves and love who we are, the true love towards others becomes real. When we have love towards ourselves and others, then we also have acceptance, and when we have love and acceptance, we are less subject to lower vibrations such as fear, anxiety, hate, anger, resentment. Do not say, how can you love yourself if you did "bad" things. You must love everything you've done. I am telling you assertively. Love yourself no matter what you've done and know that when you start to love yourself, you will stop doing "bad" things, and you will focus on the good. For some things that you could not accept, you will simply live and love yourself no matter what. I am putting the word "bad" in quotation marks, because there is nothing bad, everything is the way it was meant to be, and it will stay that way.

I used to tell my friends: "If there was no such thing as bad, then how would you know what's good, which means that that bad thing is not bad if you got something good and positive from it." You can say that I am a wise person, but that's how things are. I dare every single one of you to see if it is really like that and to yourself deeply if this Alen guy is saying the right thing for me.

Go within yourself and extract that goodness. I would even dare to say dignify yourself and observe with your consciousness that unconditional beauty that was given by God. Feel it and try to remain in that feeling for as long as you can. That is why, as a gift for all my readers, I have created a meditation that you can use to go within yourself and try to become aware of who you are and why you are here. More details can be found on page 193.

I am writing this book completely spontaneously and in the way that my memories come back to me. When I started writing it, I wanted to write it in chronological order from my childhood up to today, but it looks like that was not God's plan, so I can it write this way too. At this moment in time, I have become aware of something, so I would like to share it with you.

3.

Understanding Sex

This will be a sensitive topic for most readers. It is of course about sex.

Most people are ashamed of their sexuality and they hide those things because they are afraid that they are going to be convicted for it.

It is my opinion that this is because, when we are young, adults treat sex as something dirty and even bad. This is also connected to today's religion and its representation of sex to people. Today, they are trying to be realistic with these things. I remember in a lecture once before getting married, the words of my priest then were:

"The husband has to respect the woman in sexuality, and that is also expected from the woman. If it is any different, it leads to problems in the marriage, and even to adultery."

Those words surprised me. Usually, when I went to mass and religion class, I understood it completely differently.

Let us let go of it now and continue to the part of my life that I wanted to share with you.

It is going to be weird, and some of you might even feel the need to blame me. I want to trust you and show you that I am not ashamed of my past and the things that I have done, even though I am not proud of them. I became aware that I had a programme that I do not deserve to hear the Creator and that I am not worthy of hearing Him. I went within myself and I got an answer for where that came from.

First, I understood that it was connected to sex, and then I got that it was because of an event when I was a child, when I tried to have sex with a little girl from the neighbourhood. My dad had a car wreck, which was done up on the inside in the orchard behind our house. That is where we were hiding and tried to have sex. My brother participated as well. He was pretending to drive, and I would be "doing business" and then we would swap. As children, we just wanted to copy what the grown-ups were doing and what we saw on TV. Of course, nothing happened, but we were imitating that act and we thought it was going good for us. A human cannot fight nature. We did this a few more times until the girl got bored. She told her mother.

Yikes. My brother and I were scared. Of course, I was the main culprit for everything that happened, so I got the blame. The truth is that I started it all, but I did not force them into it. I just want to say that it is our own free will that lets us do whatever we want and nobody else must bear the consequences of our decisions. I am not saying that to justify myself, but to tell you that you all have free will and that you should not blame others and yourself for your decisions, whether they are good or bad. I was very ashamed in front of that mother when she was having a go at me. I wanted to fall through the ground and disappear. She did not use any bad words, but just her perception built up fear and resentment towards me. I did not tell you that at the time I was six years old, while they were three or four years old. We were little and immature, but we were just experimenting.

Now you may be confused because we were so little. It is my opinion that a lot of people live through something like this when they are children.

Through doing Theta Healing treatments, I have come to that realisation. Maybe not in the same way that I did, but in a similar way, I believe that you went through something like that too. Some may say that they did not, but maybe you just repressed that memory deep into your subconscious, and some will immediately say that they did, and some will not even admit that they have done such a thing. That is exactly why I am writing about my experience, and I want to show you that it is something that a lot of people live through and that it is not a taboo topic. Maybe because of that, people are ashamed of their sexuality and think that it is something dirty. Remember that after heavy work on my subconscious, I had come to the point where I thought I was not worthy of God because of sex. Well that is the way your subconscious works too.

We all come from one source and we have a lot of similarities, but on the other hand, we are all vastly different. We have different experiences and different ways of surviving them. So, you love sex and that experience. I am not saying that you should be a prostitute, I am saying that you should enjoy being with your partner and that you should get your sexuality on a new level. It is a holy ritual of love when a male and a female come to mix energies. You take over your partner and they take you over too. A part of you disappears on the spiritual level. Here I am talking about energies. We are all human beings made of energy. When you accept sex and your partner, it is like you are one in that game of merging of energies and bodies, and you will end up at the beautiful peak where for a moment you will lose your consciousness. Know that you are worthy of God at every moment regardless of sex. The Creator loves you no matter what. On the other hand, if you are prone to exchange partners or have multiple partners, it is recommended that you cleanse yourself from their energies. The best cleansing that I know is through Theta Healing, but there are other ways. It is important that you cleanse yourself from those energies and you retract fragments of your soul from those people. If you have one partner, you do not have to do that, but it is good to clean the energies every now and again. You will feel lighter, you will have more energy and you will be able to have fun just like before you had a relationship. I want to tell you to enjoy your sexuality and that you should not be ashamed of what you truly are.

Again, I am not saying that you should be sexual maniacs and attack other people, I am saying that you should accept yourself completely no matter what your sexual orientation is or your sexual wishes are. Believe me, God loves you equally. He loves you unconditionally, and if someone loves unconditionally, then that means that there are no conditions for their love.

4.

Responsibility For Your Actions

Let us go back to an event that was a break in my life after the awfully bad year of 1991. The entirety of the year was dominated by my father's sickness. 1992 came by, and I wished that it never happened. So, everything that I have told you does not compare in the slightest to the things that happened then and in the later years.

It was another beautiful day, and everything looked great and beautiful. My family, my uncle and I went to visit my mother's cousin not too far away from where we lived. A Christian holiday was held there. It was a great day, full of playing games and good times with my cousins. Everyone was happy, so happy. By so happy, I mean everyone was drinking alcohol. You will not believe this, but my father was among the people drinking along with my uncle, who thought that it was a good day for him. My uncle had come home from the war. He'd got a pass, at least that was what he said. It was mostly the men who were drinking, of course, not us kids. It was not that important that they were drinking and having a good time. It was great and nobody was too drunk. The afternoon came to an end and we had to go home, which for us was sad, but we had to listen to the adults and do as we were told. We came home and everyone went to my uncle's house. In the meantime, because of the war, there were some Muslims from a place called Jajce. It was the close family of Sakib, the husband of my grandmother. There was also a boy who was my best friend at the time. His name was Adnan. My brother, Adnan and I were playing in the yard while my father and my uncle continued drinking.

My uncle went into the house from the terrace where they were drinking, and he brought out something yellow. It looked like the clay which we used in school to make figures. Well, that clay was something far worse than a toy. It was plastic explosive. We found that out later when we saw him putting a wick into the mixture. There were two types of wicks, slow-burning ones and fast-burning ones. He was cutting the wicks in front of us kids and everyone else. He tried lighting them because they were not labelled. He decided to leave the one he thought was good. He gave us kids little bits of wicks to play with and to light on fire, while he and my father took that piece of "clay" and went off with the car.

We did not know where they went because they were lighting wicks, but some uneasy feeling awoke in me, as if I knew that something bad was going to happen. Later, we found out from the grown-ups that they went to blow up a house of an orthodox person in a place nearby called Narta. One part of me approved of the action, but on the other hand, I did not want anything bad to happen to my uncle or my father, or anyone. They did go and cause harm to somebody though. My uncle was always getting abused when he was little by this person. My uncle was very mischievous when he was younger and, at the time, the abuser was a policeman. I know that it was stupid of my uncle to do that. I told you that he was crazy.

After they left, we continued playing and we were everywhere. Night-time came and there were a lot of people sitting on a bench in front of a house. Adnan, Nino and I were there. Suddenly, we heard a large explosion. Adnan shouted, "It went off." We pretended not to hear anything that Adnan shouted in order to protect our father and uncle. Well, that explosion was the turning point of my life. Believe it or not, in the end, they did not blow up any house at all. It was something far worse.

I will never forget that one neighbour came to our house around one to two hours after the explosion. We found it weird that he was there. He walked around for a bit and then went to tell my mother:

"Ljubica, I don't know how to tell you, but something's wrong with Miro" (everyone called my father Miro because his full name was Tihomir). My mother asked him what was wrong and what had happened and then the neighbour told us what happened. When he was coming home from work as a guard at the nearby fishery, he went past a burning car. He realised that the car was my uncle's car and he saw my father being driven to the hospital by an ambulance. Unfortunately, the only part of my uncle that survived was his pelvis. Everything else was blown up by the explosive that he was preparing. Zdravko offered his condolences and said that he was sorry that he had to tell us, but he felt that he needed to do it. When my mother heard all of that, she started crying. It was not easy for me and my brother. We were sad and we started crying too. Well, how could we not when our mother was crying a lot? There was a feeling of disbelief awakening inside of me as if this was not happening. My mother was distraught and immediately went to tell my grandmother and grandfather what had happened. We stayed in the house and our mother went to the Bjelovar hospital in tears. My brother and I went to bed in tears. Honestly, I do not remember my grandparents' reaction. I did not know what was happening to them at the time. Well, how could I remember that kind of shock.

Unfortunately, yet another tragedy happened to me. When I was lying in bed, thoughts of disbelief went through my head such as "Why me? What did I do to deserve this? Why is God punishing me?" My brother and I fell asleep on the bed together and morning came. I do not remember what time my mother came home from the hospital with our godfather Josip. I do remember though that it was our godfather who came by to tell us that our uncle was no longer alive. I could not accept that. I always thought that it did not happen, and I could not accept that my uncle was gone. My father suffered heavily. He lost his right eye and right fist, and was wounded all over the right side of his body.

According to my father, they went to the house, but they had been to a few taverns along the way and they were visibly drunk. What was worse was that they were telling everyone what they were planning on doing. Finally, they were in Narta drinking their last drinks. Narta was a nearby place and its population was 50% orthodox people who were considered to be Serbs. Croatia was at war with Serbia. People in Narta were scared because their village was separated. I think the orthodox people were even more scared, because the fear was activated genetically. I mean, after all, their ancestors did come from Serbia. They'd lived in Narta for years when they were growing up, but genes are genes and you cannot escape them, but they can be changed with the help of Theta Healing. I believe that they were mutually prepared for the act that my uncle and father were planning on doing. They went from the tavern in Narta and their plan was that my father would drive and that my uncle would throw the explosive into the house. They slowly came to the place; my father stopped the car for a moment so that my uncle could get out of the car and throw the explosive. At the exact moment when my uncle sparked the wick, he collapsed back onto my father's right shoulder. My father pushed him away and shouted, "Throw it Dinko, throw it!", but Dinko was not answering. I understood that my uncle had been shot by a sniper who was waiting to resolve the matter. My father being drunk and because the left side of his body was damaged from a stroke, he could not open the car door. He said that he started panicking and he wanted to open the door as soon as possible, but he could not because his attention was on the ignited wick of the plastic explosive, which fell on the floor of the car in between my uncle's legs. Can you imagine what my father went through? He was in a car in with ½ kg of plastic explosive and it blew up. He was lucky that he is alive, even though he was sorry that it was that way. By some miracle, an ambulance passed by just at the right time. Imagine that. What are the odds of the ambulance arriving at the time of an accident? The driver and the nurse helped my father get out of the burning car. On top of everything, he also got fourth degree burns all over his body. Only a small bit of my uncle's body remained. It is amazing and lucky that my father even survived that event. Later, the doctors even acknowledged that it was phenomenal. Remember, he suffered from heart problems too. The day after the accident, we went to visit my father. We were given permission to see him for a few minutes just to see him and greet him. It was a hard moment. They were taking him to have skin grafts on his arms which were severely burnt. The encounter with him was very traumatic. He was wrapped up in bandages like a mummy. His head was wounded as was his face. When we came close to him, he said in tears that he was sorry for everything, and that we should be nice towards our mother and the house. My mother was distraught and sad. It was not easy seeing him in that state. My brother was not there, as my mother said that he was too young to see something like that, but I insisted that I be allowed to see him.

In a way I regretted that I went. It is not an image I will ever forget, but on the other hand, I wanted to see my father. Of course, a child who is 11 years old also needs courage to do something like that. The encounter was short. I told him that we would be good and that I loved him. He was in tears, even more than us, and he kept saying that he was sorry. He felt very guilty about the whole incident. It was one of the worst days in my life. It was unbelievable that these things were happening in my life.

My entire world was collapsing. There was always something bad happening, never anything good or continuous good feelings. Throughout my entire childhood, "bad luck" followed me. At least, that is what I thought back then.

Everything was good when I was at school with my friends. I would forget all the problems in my family. Then I would come home and I would see my mother crying. This happened daily after that incident. As you can imagine, I was just a child and it was difficult for me, so I can only imagine what it felt like for her, because she was an adult and she looked at things differently. She could not relax like me and forget. At least, she did not know how to do it.

A child's mind is different, so when it gets playful, it forgets the outer impacts and focuses on the playing and the fun. That is possible for grown-ups who have a choice whether they are going to wake up their inner child and stop worrying about everything. My mother did not know how to do that.

If I had not found out about Theta Healing, I think I would have been the same. When you let your inner child out, you feel free and as comfortable as a bird. You will be in the present moment and you will enjoy yourself and your environment, which you feel are a part of you and you are a part of them too. It comes to the point when a human believes that they are one with everything around them and that there are no separations. Only a person living in lower vibrations such as fear, shame, guilt and resentment finds it hard to understand that they are one with everything around them. When you are one with the nature around you, then you are at one with God. That is exactly what he is, everything that exists. The meditation of going within yourself can help you to become aware of yourself and to observe yourself from the inside. More details can be found on page 193.

Let me continue to the rest of 1992. I remember the curiosity of people who were asking me about my father daily. I did not feel comfortable talking about it, so out of decency, I said that he was alright and that he was getting better. Some even criticised him and said that he did not need to do that. Even though I shared their opinion, I did not find it easy to listen to that kind of healthy criticism coming from others about my father. I slowly resented everyone who was "against" my father. Whatever he was doing to me and however he acted towards me, I still loved him. If you love someone, then you would not like it if someone says bad things about that person, even if you know what they are saying is true. I felt sorry for him. He had lost sight in his right eye and had lost his right hand. He only saw 60% with his left eye. Imagine having that kind of father and then someone says bad things about him. I know it could be remarkably similar for you and some might even find it worse.

We buried what remained of my uncle. I was not overly sad about his death. I did not really care. He did not really love me that much and he messed around with me a lot. You know everything from before. He went away, but the feelings of resentment towards him from my mother, my family and me stayed. We used to say that everything that happened was his fault, and that if he had not been there, our father would be normal, he would not be completely healthy, but he would not be crippled. That is a fact.

By working on my subconscious and personal growth, I got an insight that we are responsible for our actions and that there is nothing else in that story. The easiest thing to do is blame someone else for your actions. I've returned to this topic because it is one of the strongest cases with people. I am telling you this, because I had a situation a few days ago that I remembered whilst I was writing this part of the book.

There were four of us, three friends and myself, because I am an intuitive person and I have cleansed myself to a high level, all our subconscious programmes came out. I was aware of my strategies and I admitted them completely, but my friends did not want to hear what I was saying to them. That is, they did not want to see their "problems". I have the need to tell you this to ease my soul. Believe me, when you tell someone something you have not told anyone before, it is already easier, and imagine the feeling when you are ready to release those kinds of incidents. It is my opinion that the release is the best technique in Theta Healing.

My mother, my brother and I spent the entire year of 1992 in the hospital with my father. The doctors were "patching" him up day by day. He used to come home for a few days and then go back to the hospital. The next year, 1993, it was the same. The rehabilitation lasted around six months. Just when I thought it was over and that he would not have to go anywhere anymore, the battle for his left eye started. The doctors said that he must have surgery done on his cornea. If the surgery succeeded, my father would be able to see more than 80% with a strong dioptre of ÷14%, which was the strongest dioptre at the time. This happened just as I thought that we were done with hospital visits and that we were not going into that place again. My parents knew something that my brother and I did not. They said that my father would go to Zagreb to get surgery done on his eye and that after the surgery he would be able to see again. I was happy because of that. I wanted him to get better as soon as possible. The day came, he went to Zagreb, and we were all excited for him to go to be healed.

There was no guarantee that the surgery would fix his eyesight, but it was a big possibility that it would work if his body accepted the new cornea. The entire family put so much hope into his recovery. He came home and we did not know anything for around a month. He went for a check-up. Imagine this, his body did not accept the new cornea.

It was as if everything in my life was dark. That is the way I saw it. There were no changes to expect. Somehow, it seemed normal to me that something bad kept happening. I would even wonder if something good would ever happen. 90% of the time, I only remember something bad always happening, only 10% of the events were good. I could even call them great because they were so rare. I did not know why it was like that, even though I was interested in it. I was looking for answers, but it looks like I did not recognise them. Unfortunately, back then, nobody was there to guide me to some higher entity and explain to me how things worked. I was always looking for those answers.

It took me 33 years to get most of the answers. Most of the answers I received from Theta Healing. No matter how dark everything was that was happening during my father's sickness, other things started to appear. There was enough money to cover basic expenses. My parents did not live a luxurious life. They were quite humble, and they did not spend money on stupid things, or fritter it away.

My father may have spent a lot of money on alcohol and spent a lot of money around taverns. Even though they were modest, there was not a lot of money and they argued because of money. I am talking about events before my father's accident. After he recovered, the arguments started again, and it was not just a few words being exchanged. They were having wars daily because of money. Believe me, it was not easy hearing my parents argue about the same thing time and time again, and using sentences like, "You spend it all. You are worthless. Everything that you are given, you spend straight away."

There were some other words too, but I would rather not mention them. I think you can predict what words they were using without me saying them. Oh yes, when it starts, it starts properly, I thought to myself. In a way, I was blaming myself for the situation. I had some ideas that could help with the flow of money in the family, but they did not acknowledge them. They just said that I do not have the right to speak about such things, and that I was still too young to suggest something to them.

Imagine what a child who is 11-12 years old would think about money when they had heard those kinds of sentences and wars. Honestly, I thought that money was the root of all evil in this world. I started hating myself and my family because of money. Well, who would not? These arguments were not just happening two or three times, they were happening constantly. That is what my daily life was like. There were times when it was peaceful just after an argument, but only if it was a tempestuous one. Sometimes, the arguments would last a long time and my parents would end up not talking for a few days. They would be sat right beside each other, being noticeably quiet and ignoring each other as if the other did not exist. To me, that ended up seeming like normal behaviour.

If I end up getting into an argument, I would not talk to that person anymore. Unfortunately, a child absorbs the patterns of behaviour completely unintentionally and later in life they are not aware of what is happening, and the situations that were once happening are happening again, just in a different sense. There were some days when they did not argue, but they still provoked each other. My father was the one who provoked my mother more, but she did not always react. I also think that I leaned towards my father's side. He was sick, he could not walk alone and what was worse was that he could not see properly. My mother could do all those things, and she often worked to earn just enough money to survive and so that my father could still go to the hospital. My father had a pension which was not enough for all of us and his treatment.

I used to ask myself why we could not be rich and have things the way rich people do. Those people always fascinated me. Why? Because I saw that, in poverty, a person hates more, resents more and blames more. I thought that rich people were better and more advanced. That was my opinion as a child, but that has changed now. I remember one bit of good news at the time, my father decided that we are going to get a lassie dog. My brother and I could not wait for us to get it. At the time, there was a movie about a smart dog called Lassie and a boy, the dog's owner. We were delighted when the dog came home. He was black and white. He was happy that he came to a family and I was happy that we got him. We named him Johnny. That dog awakened hope in me that I would be like the boy from the movie, that I would be happy and that my life would take a turn for the better. A child's mind can imagine anything. It is even possible to make things real if we clean our subconscious. Unfortunately, my subconscious was not clean back then and neither was my parents' subconscious. By clean, I mean that it did not have any negative vibrations such as hate, resentment, guilt and anger. Believe me, today, I know what it is like to have a clean subconscious and I know what I am talking to you about. I wanted to say that if someone had told me back then that my subconscious was not clean and if they had told me how to clean it, I would have done it straight away and I would have gone on a path towards a much better life. At the same time, because my subconscious was the way it was, nothing I wanted came true. I wanted a happy family, a lot of money, a nice car, a nice house and a nice yard. On the other hand, if I had cleaned my subconscious back then, I would have helped myself to achieve that, and I would also have been able to help my family.

With Theta Healing, you can clean those genetic shortcomings. When you look at that concept, it is the most powerful thing that has come to this world. It came with a reason too. Look at how much suffering, tormenting, wars and fights that happen around you. Is it not time for everything to begin to decline and to stop? People think that God has abandoned us, but it is the total opposite. God is sending us people who are ready to help us. He sent us Theta Healing and many other techniques. It is not all nonsense, as there is a reason for everything including the different techniques that have appeared in the past few decades.

In another part of the book, I will explain in detail what Theta Healing is. I could do it now, but I want to show you what my life was like in the past.

So, my dog Johnny grew, and I was happy with him. My brother loved him too, but I "adopted" him. He was my dog. I just wanted to be that happy boy who happily runs in the fields with his smart dog. Sometimes, it really was like that. We really did use to run in the fields through the grass. We used to roll all over through the grass. They were some of the best moments of my childhood. In a way, it was an escape from reality, because I pretended that I lived someone else's life. I did not know better. Often people relate to some character in a movie or TV series. It is as if in that way they can live how they really want. That is okay in some way for these characters to guide us, but it's not good to make energetic bonds with those things or people.

I want to say that it is good to have an imagination, but on the other hand, it is not good that we make bonds with things that do not exist. Imagination is the actual thing that creates, but only when we let go of what we want. As a child, I wanted to have a good life and to be happy with my family, but nothing went according to plan. My imagination was not to blame. That is the way that my soul decided to live so that I can now show you that changes are possible. It is not just for you. I was gaining a lot of experience as well.

I am thinking about the fact that, today, I am a parent of a child who I love so much that it is unexplainable, and I try my best to not do the things to him that my parents did to me. Even if I stopped at that, it would have been a lot. However, my soul wants to make something more from pure compassion. My soul wants to help all the people who want to help themselves, who want happiness, success, joyfulness, prosperity and whatever they want. I know that that is possible, and I believe in you. It is important that you believe in yourself in the same way that I believed in myself and in the end it came true. The truth is that I needed time, but I was gathering certain experiences along the way. Everything comes at the right time, and it is necessary to believe that everything is going to be the way you want it to be. Johnny brought a certain type of joy into the family. It was as if everything was different. My father did not see him, but somehow, he was still happier. He did not spend his days in loneliness. He was often alone as my brother and I were in school and my mother worked around the village. My grandparents were doing their own work in the fields and with the animals that we had. So, Johnny did not bring joy just to me, but he also brought joy to my father as he was company for him.

It was obvious that my father was not too happy, and I often saw him crying and mourning. He was alone with his thoughts, which was difficult. He was confronting himself. This is not something that he told me, but because my whole life I have been intuitive, I simply knew that. Intuition is exactly what we are all born with, but later we supress it because we are not taught that we have it and that it is possible for people to have intuition. People just say that it is an instinct. It is not an instinct; it is pure intuition. You know when you just know that something is the way you think. The problem in everything is the fact that there are other people who do not want to admit that you know something more than them, so they deny it instead of finding the truth about themselves. I suppressed my intuition deep into myself, but with Theta Healing, I got it back, and now I believe in myself and in my intuition. Intuition is conscious living and connection with the Creator. At least, that is my opinion. Later in the book, I will talk more about it, because I have an interesting story on how I got in touch with my intuition and when I realised that I had it.

Later that year, we got another pet in the house. One gloomy and wet day, I went out to gather snails so that I could make some money for myself. Johnny was at home. Whilst I was looking for snails, I heard a weird noise, but it was not a bird, as I first thought. When I came closer to the noise, I saw a fawn lying in the nettles, a baby deer. I did not know what happened to the mother, but she was nowhere around the fawn. My conclusion was that hunters had killed the mother overnight, because a deer does not leave her fawn. I felt sorry for the little one and I took it home with me. I was not looking for snails anymore. What I found was worth much more than snails. It was like another child movie in which a group of children found a fawn in the nature and protected it from a hunter. Interesting, how my life was just like those movies about a dog and a deer. I do not know how, but my wishes came true when I watched the movies. In the span of a year, I had a dog and now my own deer. I brought the fawn home, and the family was also happy with my find. Of course, I was happy and proud of myself for what I'd found. My grandmother immediately found a bottle so that we could feed the fawn with some cow's milk. We sat and talked about what we were going to name him, but I already had a name in mind, Jelenko. So that is what we called the fawn. It suited him and it was also the name of the fawn from the movie. I was so thankful to God for sending those two creatures into my life and in the same year. In difficult times, they were such good comfort, not just to me, but to the whole family.

I ended up liking Jelenko more than Johnny. Johnny was playful and he always jumped and drooled everywhere, but Jelenko was calm, nice and cuddly. As Jelenko grew, he became smarter and more attached to me and my family. He slept with us in the house. He acted like a human, except that he just did not talk. Wherever I went, he went with me. He was never too far away from me and, whenever I called him, he would immediately come to me. My heart swells because I am aware that God sent me Johnny and Jelenko to comfort me in the bad situations that I had. I believe that it was the same with my family too. They also needed something to comfort them in any way possible. The two brought a new energy to the house and I no longer worried over the regular arguments. For when my parents did argue, I had someone to hug. You will say that I had a brother, but remember that I did not like him a lot, at least subconsciously, and I did not see that I could hug him at those times. It is different from what we want consciously and it's different to what our subconscious expects us to do. I subconsciously resented and blamed my brother for everything bad that ever happened to me, so I did not really want to hug him and get comfort that way. That is why I had Johnny and Jelenko. I remember their warmth and heart beats. It is remarkable how a dog and a fawn were friends in our family. By that, I mean with the general situation in the house and all the negative energy that was everywhere, it was a miracle. Now, I believe in miracles and I believe in the fact that a miracle did happen then. Imagine a dog and a fawn being in the place that has little to no love in it. The dog was older than the fawn when we first got him. Usually, if they were brought up together from when they were babies, it would have been normal, but for a wild animal to enter the dog's space and for there to be no fights is incredibly beautiful. We were not aware of the beauty that was happening, or to be exact, the miracle of nature and God united. Now, I am truly thankful for that experience and the fulfilled wish. That fulfilled wish helped the burden of my childhood and it gave me a positive memory in life. The positive memory was not just important to me, it was the feeling of comfort that I had. It was somehow easier to live, no matter the fights that I heard.

There was an interesting situation that happened in the house that nobody could explain. When we were sleeping in the house, Johnny was sleeping in the living room because I did not have my own room at the time, and Jelenko was sleeping in the stable. He was almost full grown, so my parents did not let him be in the house at night. Johnny was allowed and he was with us overnight, but during the day, they were together in the house. Now to the point. It was an ordinary night in which nothing special was happening, or so we thought. In the morning when we woke up, the living room door was closed, and Johnny was in the hallway. It would be easy to explain if he opened the door on his own and went out, but the door was closed. We were all confused because nobody in the family closed the door. How did Johnny open the door and then close it?

That is when I first started to believe in ghosts. That was my only logical explanation. That is when I started thinking that they were the reason for all our tragedies and the fights in the family. I had a feeling that we were the only ones in the village who argued. Today, I see that it is not like that, but back then, I believed different things. I think I was looking for someone to blame for our situation and it was a very weird situation. There were stories that a man once lived on the spot where our house was built. Allegedly that man was given to be killed by my great-grandfather Josip during World War I, because he was an elder in the village. I had not heard any nice stories about him. People just did not like him because he collected crops for the country. That was pure robbery, but it was like that back then and he was just a person doing work for the country. It is not important what the country was like, what is important is my great-grandfather. I found some logic in everything. I believed that everything bad that was happening to me was because of the actions of my great-grandfather and that we were cursed. I think I was close to the truth, because there is a law of cause and effect, which means that every cause has its own consequences. It all depends on the situation. That law of the Universe is direct, but it is also righteous. It is that law that "punishes" people, not God. Considering my great-grandfather did all kinds of things, I am not surprised that we really were "punished". My great-grandfather lived a rich life and he did not have any major problems. All of his problems he took with him when he died. But he left them in my DNA. It was the genes that were causing all the problems in my life, and it was the thing I fixed the most with Theta Healing. With this technique, you can indeed fix genetic shortcomings, conditions, curses, contracts and spells in the genes. Whatever our ancestors did that was bad in their lives, it stays written in the DNA. That is how things are, but that is why we have this marvellous technique where we can change the genetic shortcomings and much more. We never really found out what happened to Johnny that night when he "closed" the door.

At the time, me and my brother found out about summoning ghosts. You know that when children think of something, they just want to do it. We summoned ghosts in the school too. We drew a shape of a person and wrote the alphabet around him, and there were also two words, "yes" and "no". In the place where the heart should be on the person, we stuck a needle with a string which was held by the pointer finger and thumb. The summoning was done just by words:

"Spirit, Spirit, are you there? If you are, turn this needle to yes."

Believe it or not, the needle turned to yes. We were amazed and shocked, because it really happened. We did not do anything like that in school, because we were scared. Not all children were daring and brave. You could say that they were just smarter than my brother and me. The two of us repeated the same thing at home. I remember that some ghost did respond and that he gave us his name. I do not remember the name, but it really happened. It is interesting how things to do with ghosts started happening at the same time. Firstly, the thing with the dog and my house, then after that, we started summoning them. I do not know why that was happening to this day. My assumption is that they tried to contact us to get help to go into the light. It was not necessary because there are some bad ghosts who try their best to do wrong to people. I do not remember if the ghosts we contacted were nice or not, but as things carried on, I believe that we contacted a good ghost who tried to help us. Either way, my brother and I were very scared of everything, and we threw that paper away. It was a period of our lives when we tried all kinds of things out of curiosity. Of course, we were children and that was a taboo topic which the adults used to scare us.

<u>Warning!</u>

Do not try to do what I just wrote, for your own safety.
Do not play with the world of ghosts, because they can harm you.

The problem was that the adults were letting us know that something does exist, but they were not exactly sure that something supernatural really existed. We were very curious to find out if it was true, and we witnessed that it was. Later, we stopped doing things like that. We were scared, and who would not be when doing something like that?

That period of life was unclear, and I must admit that a lot of the things are hard to remember. I do not have an answer why. It is interesting that I stopped writing this book when I came to this part. It took me a few months to begin realising this part. I believe that everything will start going ahead and that I will succeed in showing you my life and the possibilities of change in life. Believe me, if I did not have the need to help you, I would have stopped writing this book.

Somehow, in my soul, I know that this is the right thing to do and that it will help other souls to become aware, so they can see that it is not so dark in life. There are many light points in life. You just need to become aware of them and know that they are here and now. Every light situation comes just once, I mean a specific situation. If it comes once, I am inviting you to enjoy it. Be joyful like children, wake up the child within you, and enjoy and play. That is the purpose of living, that is the point, the essence. Even hard situations are "hard" because our mind registers them like that and not because they are hard. Remember when you were a child and something was hard, you spent a few minutes in that state and then you continued playing again. This is what I dare you to do – to try to play in life and feel the joy in your hearts. I know you can do it and that you can dare to do it. That is why you should start now and grasp your moment in life.

Now, I am currently writing this story about my past to the present, so that I can show you how hard it can be for someone in their life and how much personal choice can change things to whatever you want. I know someone will say, "Easy for him to say that as he got the chance to change." My dear people, every day we get a chance and any help we need. It is up to us if we want to accept it or not. God does not come personally and help us like some elder with a big beard – well that is how I imagined him. God comes to you every day, through other people. He is in all of us, he is everything that exists. I cannot stop admiring that kind of perfection and creation. Believe me, if you ever need help, he is always there to help. The only condition that exists is that you do not look for a way that he will help you, but just pray for help and help will come.

It will come just as you ask, but you do have to be patient. You should just let go and believe that he is here for you and that you are worthy of him helping you. Because if somebody loves you unconditionally, then it is the Creator. I am writing this with confidence because I lived through countless miracles and answers to my prayers. Through prayer, I started writing this book. I came to a moment when the fear of success and responsibility dragged me away from my writing. My soul still decided to overcome the fear and, of course, if all my bodies (physical, ethereal, spiritual) had not aligned themselves, I would not have started writing. That is why we have a choice. I had it now too. Somehow, I feel that it is necessary for all of this to be put on paper, because if I manage to motivate at least one person to change their way of life and to turn to God, I have done a massive thing. The Earth begs for help. I do not know why I am writing this, all I know is that everything that comes to my mind is being transferred onto paper with my hand, so forgive me if I talk about myself and the past and God and my opinions.

5.

Keep Going No Matter How Hard It Is

I will continue with my past now, because hard times were coming. That is what marked my life the most. So, I will continue with my "unlucky" life. Unlucky is in quotation marks because now I know that that life brought me here where I am today. It even gave me happiness and wealth. I was talking to you about Jelenko, and the saddest thing is that Jelenko was a year old at the time. My family told us children that they were going to let Jelenko free, out into nature to mate and to continue living. Unfortunately, the truth is that my grandparents killed Jelenko and put the meat in the freezer. I found that out over a year after it happened. Finding that out made me so sad, because I remembered the times when my grandmother served food on the table. As a child, I even asked what it was and they told me that it was pigeon soup. You can imagine how I felt when I found out that I had eaten someone that I deeply loved. It is not just that I loved him, I know that he loved me too. Of course, life keeps going and it is necessary to accept the facts and to keep moving on, no matter how hard it is. I am telling you this because life is not easy, and it will put you on your knees quite often. Do not give up, but be tough and persistent. In the way that this book is tragic throughout then with a good ending, I will continue with the worst thing that happened in my life.

There are many people who may have experienced worse things than me and, if you did, believe me, I sympathise with you. A person who lives a hard life with compassion feels the suffering of other people.

It was Christmas Eve 1995. As a child, I loved Christmas. Most of the time, my parents were in a jolly mood and, for me, that meant a break from getting punished and getting beaten, which happened quite often because of my mischievous nature and unnecessary responsibility for my brother. That day, my brother and I were firing firecrackers in our small village. We got most of them as gifts and we bought some too, unfortunately with money stolen from the family. "What kind of Christmas would it be without firing firecrackers?", were our thoughts before we got them. Times have changed and thank God that there is less of that. I know that some of you might not agree with firing them, especially, if it is children who are underage who are setting them off. You need to understand that this was the way we grew up and that our minds were conditioned in a bad way, you could say. That is why I am encouraging you, if you want to hear with your hearts, to not fire any kinds of fireworks during the holidays, but to celebrate another way. Celebrate life, celebrate family, celebrate the abundance in your life through songs and joy. Imagine how many animals are stressed and even die because of the noise that fireworks produce. They are living creatures that understand and feel everything, but they do not speak our language.

So, now I will talk about the hardest part of my life and my first contact with death. Somehow some things cannot be changed because they are marked the way they are. Some call that fate or destiny. Our entire life is not our destiny, because with our decisions, we change the reality in which we live. The best way for us to live is to listen to our feelings. You know that feeling in your gut, well that is it. If something is wrong, it tells you everything. You just need to learn how to understand that feeling through observing yourself and the situations when that feeling appears. I cannot seem to start writing what happened that Christmas Eve. It's as if I am trying to avoid facing myself with everything and writing everything that happened.

You might not believe it, but I had to stop writing the book again, right at this point. Then three years later, I started again and I believed that I would finish writing it to the end.

Because we were firing firecrackers, we did not tell our parents where we were going and because we spent one or two hours firing the firecrackers at our neighbours, I became worried. It was already dark, and we knew that we were going to get punished when we got home, unless I thought, I went home and told my parents where we were. I told my friends and my brother that I was going home to tell my parents where we were. My brother said that he was coming with me. I knew that if he came that we would not be going back out. I tried to convince him that he should stay there, but he was insistent. It is interesting. I was very persistent, which I still am today, and I tried a third time, but he still decided to come with me. He did not tell me what was going through his head, and I would love to know the reason why today. I believe that it was the fear of our parents, because they were extremely strict. We headed home, which was around 200 metres away, and on the way home, we saw our next-door neighbour. A small path separates our houses. He went out with a gun to shoot it to celebrate. He was a soldier in his early 30s. He was amazing to us, a hero. Now we were firing again, just with a real gun. We stood aside as he shot with his AK-47. Our parents heard him shoot, so our mother was looking out through the window some 5 metres away and our father went out of the main gate, which was 10-15 metres away. That is when the neighbour said to our father, "Mirć, (Tihomir, people called him many different variants of his name out of friendship) look at this."

The neighbour took out a handmade gun that he had brought from war. He filled it up with one bullet like a hunting rifle that hunters use to shoot birds and shot it in the air with a powerful bang. We were all laughing and were astonished at the sound. That is when the neighbour put in the second bullet. The positions were like this, Nino was one metre in front of the neighbour, I was beside the neighbour, a boy named Ivan was four or five metres on the left of the neighbour, my mother was at the window and my father was walking towards us to see better up close that "miracle" of a gun.

The neighbour put a bullet in the barrel and when he was closing the gun, it went off. I will never forget that. The last sound my brother made was "auuuu". Nino collapsed and I was stunned. A panic started, but I came back to my senses and ran for the phone. I called the ambulance to come help Nino. It was total pandemonium. My parents were there around Nino and they were crying.

The neighbour brought out his car and we put Nino into the back seat. I decided to go with them. The neighbour drove extremely fast, so fast that Nino's body fell off the seat a few times. Because I had seen in movies how to do CPR, I tried to do it on Nino. I tried a few times, but nothing happened. I saw the gunshot wound, which was exactly where his heart was. There were small holes around from the smaller fragments of the bullet. When I was trying to do CPR, all you could hear is a gurgling sound, like the sound you make when you put a straw into water and then blow air through it. I was calm and I believed that Nino was going to be okay. Everyone was saying he would not, but I wished for a miracle. Some 15km away, we saw the ambulance, so we then transferred him into the ambulance. I was with him in the back. I will never forget that sound, as if he were calling for help. Unfortunately, there was no help. It did not matter that we drove through red lights. The doctors took Nino's lifeless body into a room. I stood outside with the neighbour. My parents came with our godfather Josip.

That was when the shock and disbelief hit me. I could not accept what had just happened. I kept repeating that he was going to stay alive, he was going to be ok. I do not remember when and how the doctors came out to tell us the bad news. I think that they talked to my mother.

Yes, Nino died that Christmas Eve, right on the spot. Shot straight through the heart, with no help at all.

We came back home, and I do not remember that night very well. It was all a blur. I remember the next morning though. I was in tears sitting against the bedroom wall. I cried and cried, and I tried to believe that it was just a bad dream and that the doctors were going to call home to tell us that they had made a mistake and he was alive. I had such a difficult time trying to process everything that happened between me and him. All the bad things I had ever done to him came to my mind as a vision, followed by crying and mourning.

So, on Christmas of 1995, when you usually celebrate Jesus's birthday, I mourned and regretted all my actions towards my brother. The lesson is that you should act and love someone as if it were your last day alive, but not just yours, the other person's as well. This was the first time I had experienced a death in the family, although, I did see one neighbour hanging from a beam in her stable. That was also a trauma that frightened me for years, because at night in the dark, I would run fast passed that house, because she was haunting it as she did not find her peace. Some may say that I am mistaken; however, I am talking about my feelings and experiences.

Let me go back to the deaths in my family, because there were more in the future. If there were not any alternative methods of healing, I would most probably be in a psychiatric hospital. When you experience the death of someone very close to you, that you were negative towards, all the bad words or actions will feel very real. We need to realise and accept everything as an experience. Knowing that the person that passed does not want us to suffer. Of course, this was my experience, although I believe that this happens to all of us. I believe that this happens because we must learn our lessons. We become wiser and act differently next time with other family members or people in general. We need to love others like this could be our last day together, truly in our hearts, that way we will live a richer, happier and easier life. As people say: "life flies in front of your eyes." That is why we are here, to learn from each other. We are not here to suffer. Suffering comes from your mind, and if we are in our mind too much, then suffering is guaranteed. Our heart has wisdom and knowledge, so if we are in our heart, we have trust in life and we act in a way that we do not hurt others.

There are of course healthy boundaries when even though we are in the heart, we do not let other people use us. The healthy boundaries are represented by honest talking with yourself at the beginning of a situation and by an honest act if it comes to a misunderstanding. It is particularly important to be able to say "no" to people and situations. When you get the chance, listen to the emotions which talk to us from other people. Believe me, even though there are skilled manipulators and liars who can cover up the truth, they can do it for a short while, but sooner or later the truth is revealed. Lies and deception cannot lead you to a good life without suffering. The truth always wins and it will be shown to you. It is just a matter of time. I must be honest, I have encountered a lot of people who were skilled manipulators. Today, I carry things much more easily, and I notice the patterns much better through observing life and the people around me.

How do you defend yourself from those people? Be as honest as you can and say what does not suit you, and then just get away from that person. You should know that that person does not serve you for your highest good, no matter what the person says. Words and acts must be as one, so that basically people's actions must be the same as what they say. If that does not happen, it means that they are lying to you. Real friends, partners or any other person will not lie to you if they are honest with you.

Forgive me for wandering off again. My heart decided to write like that. I did not mention that the departure and mourning for Nino was not so easy. Later in my life when I thought that everything was okay, it really was not. When working on Theta Healing, I found out that whenever I would come to that event, my mind would completely fall apart, and I would go into a state of crying and enormous sadness. That was a sign that my heart was getting rid of that sadness. I did not tell you that now, a few years later, I see the purpose and meaning of why I did not write the book. I am now more mature, even though I would not consider my life perfect. Why? I will tell you a secret. A perfect life does not exist the way we want it to exist. Perfection in this world is possible and we can find it in nature. In nature everything is created in perfect order, but what is the difference between our life and natures, is a life without expectations and a life that just exists and that shows us how God actually functions.

What actually happened was that my jealousy created those kinds of situations and that my mother was not aware of her actions. But it was a projection from my jealousy into her, because sometimes people are acting for us and they are not aware of what they are doing, because they are proving to us that what we think is the truth.

This is a false reality and most people are living this way without knowing what is happening. We have to question ourselves often, is this current situation that I am in, coming from me or it is something from them? The best way to recognise those things is our own emotional reaction towards the situation. If we emotionally react on something then it is our own subconscious program. If there is no emotional reaction then it is something from them If we are not in our minds and if we completely connect to our heart and emotions. A perfect life from the mind does not exist, because it is planned, but life is not planned, it is created.

I will give you an example. If you want to create a house in your life, the house will come, but God does not know what kind of house you want. That means that you need as many details as you can to describe that house through a vision and emotions. When I attracted things into my life, I understood just one thing. I would love to have a house from a picture, I would love to have an apartment in

Zagreb, I would love to have that kind of car. All of it came true, because I was not tied to profit, I just let God decide if he wants to bring it into my life. I believe that a lot of people are trying to manipulate the law of attraction. Manipulation comes from the mind. The mind also plans, so you do not get the things you want in your life. In all honesty, what do we really need to live? Is it houses, yachts, cars, apartments, weekend houses? Today, I would say that what is important in life is to have peace, joy, pleasure, love, compassion and forgiveness towards yourself and others.

If you ever manage to go through personal growth with alternate methods and bring yourself into order to have a positive view on life, everything you ever wanted and wished for will become your reality. I will be a bit critical to the people who preach the law of attraction and I will say just this. Your life and the way you treat your family leaves an image of you. If you are in the energy of arguments in the family that is when you are in the mind. From the mind without connecting to the heart, we cannot create anything special. If we are in the heart and connected with our mind, that's when life can be brought into order. Before that, roll up your sleeves and see for yourself what you want and how honest you are to yourself and others. Believe me, an honest life brings you closer to God because he is indeed the truth. The truth is that love is everywhere, but we have our programmed minds to absorb everything in our environment, both good and "bad".

Think about what I said in the book about movies, and how it dawned on me that I got a dog and a deer because I wished with the feelings of a child. Today, movies are not the way they used to be. There are a lot of bad words and situations. When I watched horror movies in the past, my life was a horror, but not in a literal way. Everything was going downhill, and I never got God's blessing. Why? When we watch dark movies, TV series, hate speeches, murders, we are giving our creative energy to dark and heavy energies. Instead of creating life the way we want, we sit in front of a TV (a glowing box) wasting the time which we could invest into creating our realities. The same is what people do today. We teach children to play videogames in which subliminal messages are hidden. Those children grow up like robots in front of a computer or console. When I was a child, there were just toys and sand. That is why poor children are different from rich children, because their parents can afford everything and, by doing that, they are tying the children to material things while they should be tying them to what is important, which is unity, love, connection and playing with their parents.

In today's age, people work too hard to earn money and they are separated from their families because of that money. I am not saying that you need to stop, but you need to strike a balance. Everything goes around the balance. It is not good to be obsessed with money, but it is also not good to be totally against money. What is important is to listen to your feelings and observe your thoughts. If we are sorry that we missed some activity of our child, another time we will act differently. The decision is up to you. That is why my life today is not perfect, because it requires a lot of personal discipline, observing myself and others around me to bring everything to be right in love. Unconditional love towards someone who is not acting their best towards you, or who is acting badly towards you can help you in hugely if you remain in unconditional love. That means love your close ones like you love yourself, no matter how and what way they do. We are here to learn to love and accept each other. If you do your part, the person who is bad will change or disappear from your life. That is my personal experience from observing life for a few years.

I am writing all of this because I honestly care what people on this planet are and become, because we all come from one source no matter what our religion, our nationality or our race. We are all here to learn from each other without judging each other.

Somehow, it is becoming harder to write again because I am approaching the part where I face death in the family for the second time. Before we get there, I would like to say why the subtitle of the book is "Through Love and Forgiveness".

I did not say what happened with my neighbour after he accidentally killed my brother. Because we were good friends, and he was a young man, my parents decided that they would not press charges against him, as it would have been another life ruined. Honestly, of all the bad lessons that my parents gave me through their arguments, and through beating and blaming me, that lesson was the best. That is when I started to learn how to forgive someone who gives you a bad experience. I have a feeling that my parents did that for peace and for what other people would have said.

I had a few treatments on myself to forgive subconsciously, because we think that we have forgiven someone, but our deep subconscious thinks differently. Unfortunately, in a few words, my neighbour did not treat me like a good neighbour and a boy who had lost his brother to him. Later, I stopped blaming him. Instead, I looked deep into myself for the answer to what did I do to cause his behaviour to be like that. That means that I took responsibility for my life. So, thanks to us, our neighbour stayed working in the military, because my mother was a witness as her lawyer asked her. I would love it if he would honestly say thank you for what we did, because I can see that my mother was strongly affected by it and that she still suffers from depression. Unfortunately, she is not open to alternative forms of healing, so I am unable to help her as I would like. Things are like that because some souls decide to suffer more when they have that kind of experience.

Unfortunately, my mother had an exceedingly difficult life and what is coming to me now is that she is getting karma from her past lives. Yes, you heard me, past lives. Past lives exist and always will exist. Today, I am so convinced about it that nobody could tell me otherwise. I had around three months of battle with my mind because I grew up in a Christian family. I would not want to change anybody's mind or contradict their beliefs. You all have the right to believe and research your truth. So, just love, forgiveness and acceptance brought me to a state of unity with myself and, of course, everyone else. It simply is not an easy thing, because you need a lot of honesty and to let go of others so that they can live their life the way they want to. Because my intuition works often, I can see the solution for a lot of people, but a lot of them do not want to hear me or do not want to act in that way.

That is when it is necessary for me to draw the line and move away from that situation. I am still moving on with some difficulty. Believe me, this is not easy to write. I think it seems that way when we imagine it, like many things in life, but it is not.

It was the 15th of March 1996. It was an ordinary morning, and everything was as usual. My father Tihomir was listening to the radio. He was blind in one eye and saw around 70% with glasses through the other one, and he had lost his right arm. My father did not follow his diet and ate everything that was bad for his heart. He also had pills for his heart. He had a heart attack that afternoon. We called the local doctor, and she came as soon as she could and treated him. My father was better after she came. I was scared when it all happened and sad that I would lose my father. I did not care about how he acted towards me in the past, I still loved him. He had stopped beating me, but really, he could not have even if he wanted to. I remember that I loved cars and I borrowed an album of images from 1995 of all the car models that came out that year. My father was with me and he wanted to look at it, so I gave it to him. Later when it was dark, he said he was going to bed in the neighbouring room. The doors were opened between the living room where I slept and the bedroom where he slept. As he was leaving, I continued looking at the album and some overpowering feeling of sadness came over me. It was a feeling as if my father would never see that album again. Tears started pouring out of my eyes and then my mind unlocked and I continued reading about cars.

My mother was working all day at a neighbour's house preparing wood for winter. She came home afterwards. She just ate some soup for dinner because the neighbour said that my father did not feel well that day. When she went to check up on my father, he was covered in sweat and he told her that he was going to die. She called me over and that is when the chaos started. He had another heart attack. My mother was shouting to go bring my grandparents into the room. I ran to get the phone to call the ambulance. They said that they could not come this far and that we should drive him to hospital. We were around 18km away from the nearest hospital. I immediately called our neighbour Ivo, because my mother had worked at his house all day. I went back into the room where my mother was with my grandparents and my half-dead father. My grandfather was doing something with his hands and he even tried pumping my father's heart, in a way which is usually done to a small calf when it is born. He did not know any better and had nowhere to learn how to do first aid. I did not know 100% either, but I'd seen it in movies, so I tried to do it too by massaging his heart and doing CPR. With every breath of mine, my father made a sound as if he were going to throw up. He was on his back and I desperately tried reviving him. Every time, he made the same sound. I was thinking to myself, "Why he is not coming back?" I prayed quietly to myself for him to come back so I would not have to be without him, but unfortunately, he decided to go.

Our neighbour came and we somehow got my father into the car. My mother went with my father and neighbour to the hospital as quickly as they could. My grandparents and I stayed at home full of tears and disbelief. We waited for my mother to call us from the hospital and give us the news. She did not call us, but she came home in tears and told us that there was no help, that he had died. Again, I could not believe that my life was so cursed. At least, that is what I thought to myself at the time. I was left without my brother and my father in the span of just three months. Once again, I felt sadness, guilt and heavy mourning. I was trying process how I was bad to my father, how I did not listen to him when he said something and, what was worse, that we had not looked at the album together until the end, in a moment of mutual understanding. I felt remorse and I blamed myself for everything. I hated myself for everything that happened, as if I had started all of it. I asked myself, "Why did the doctor not send him into a hospital straight away?" He already had heart disease.

Why?

Today, I know that everything happens for a reason and that I do not have the right to decide who dies and who does not, and that I cannot point fingers at people to blame someone else for what is going on in my life. Because my father was blind and had lost an arm, and had lost his younger son, he was carrying too much sadness because of everything. After Nino died, he cried often. That sadness and mourning took my father away. Why? Because the heart, lungs and the blood system are directly connected to sadness. Those emotions harm people and can bring disease to those systems. This statement is general because we are multidimensional beings and we are extremely complicated to understand. There are various emotions that are missing with all that sadness and mourning. You could say that humans are like perfect robots. A robot that programs his mind from birth to seven or eight years of age and, for some, a bit later too. The birth to eight years age span is filled with key moments which create the "super programme" or the entity that people call the ego. Later when we grow up, that programme causes many situations that we are not aware of happening.

Forgive me, but I will go back to the beginning of my life and I will announce something wrong with modern healing methods that people teach is not the way that they teach you. All of what I wrote has sent me back to a time when during a treatment, I entered my subconscious and I went back to the moment when I entered the womb. I cannot guarantee this, but the feelings and visions were clear, and I usually do not get visions. My intuition was sound-based and feeling-based, but then I had a vision. I was in a beautiful cloud that was light grey and pinkish in colour. That is when I was making a deal with the Creator on what I was supposed to do in this world. The Creator is just energy and we cannot touch Him. But we can feel Him and hear Him through the little voice in our heads. There is also the voice of your ego, so you need to learn to listen. The voice of the Creator comes to me from the back of my right ear. That is how I recognise it from my ego. The Creator will tell you only positive things and will not make you do something bad to yourself. That is the voice when you hear "Don't go there" and you stubbornly go there anyway, and you end up in some bad situation.

Back to entering my mother's womb. Yes, I remember it, it is cut deep into my memory after that treatment. From that beautiful cloud of easiness, love and freedom, I entered some cold and dark place. I did not even feel welcome. There was a lot of hate, resentment and guilt. I felt very constricted, and I even started hating the Creator for sending me there, even though it was my decision. So as much as I remember, the moment I entered the womb, my heart started beating. This means that the soul is ready at that moment, because the heart is developed at the time, but according to modern medicine, it develops after that. Believe me, a child hears everything, and it feels all the mother's emotions, and I mean all of them. I remember that my father yelled at my mother a lot and even beat her when I was in the womb. I gathered all those feelings and what is most important is that I felt guilty for it all. I wanted to check if all of this was true after the treatment, so I asked my mother. My mother never contradicted what I asked. You could say that she was surprised at how I knew it all. There were times when I remembered being born. It was one of the hardest experiences during Theta Healing. I heard in the womb how my mother was screaming, and I felt her pain. I honestly did not want to come out, as I was done with everything because I was in an unfamiliar environment for nine months. My mother wanted a girl, and I knew that. I did not want to disappoint her. Later, I had problems with choosing my gender because of this, even though I have never had sex with a man. Back to the hospital. I was stubborn and I did not want to come out, but my mother kept pushing and she had major pains during childbirth. I was her first child. In the end, I did not have enough power to hold myself in, so I flew out. I remember I hated the first breath I took, and I had an unfriendly response to the element of air. I remember the doctor grabbed me and gave me to the nurse. The nurse cleaned me, and I cried. She wanted to give me to my mother, but my mother was angry and, imagine this, she rejected me in the very beginning of my life. Remember what I said about the way my mother acted. I would say today that she subconsciously hated me and that she hated me for all the pain she went through while giving birth to me. I would also say that she was punishing herself because any pain that happens to us is a sign that something is wrong inside of us, emotionally. After she rejected me, the nurse put me on a bed beside her. It is hard to describe the bed, but I could draw it. It was like the children's beds for changing diapers. In the moment when she rejected me, I had so much anger towards my mother that I opened my eyes and told the leader of the treatment that if my mother were there right now, I would push her from the building and kill her. Imagine how much hate and anger I had towards my own mother. Now, it is clear to me why our relationship before I started healing myself was not healthy. We constantly argued and now everything was obvious. After the treatment ended, I let go of all the anger, resentment and guilt towards myself, my mother and the Creator. I learnt my lesson that the element of air exists, but it is up to us whether we want to accept and love it. My mother knew no better, and she had a hard time in labour. I had compassion for her then. The Creator did not do anything other than be around us, as it was not his top priority.

You see the way we are? We are so complicated and how easy it is to look at a situation from just one angle. That is why it is best to look at every situation with acceptance that it was meant to be that way and forgive every participant of the situation, but mostly, you need to forgive yourself. If you blame yourself, hate yourself or whatever you hate then, you are also blaming the God inside of you because you are a part of God deep inside of your heart and you are also a part of his plan to learn and grow in this world in love, peace, acceptance and compassion through forgiveness. Jesus said: "Love your closest ones as you would love yourself."

This means that we cannot love anybody honestly if we do not love ourselves.

There is an exercise that can be difficult for some, but it is possible. Every morning when you wake up, look at yourself in the mirror and say, "I love you (say your name)." Look into your eyes and be honest. Witness how the world around you will start changing right in front of your eyes within two weeks to 40 days. Unfortunately, everything that I lived through, later reflected onto my family, but I will talk about that closer to the end. That is why I decided that because I have just one son, Leonardo, who I feel suffered more than me, and if I ever have more children in my life, I will use the Hawaiian tradition. The tradition is a bit weird to the modern world, but through all the wisdom that I have gathered during my life, it sounds great. In the Hawaii, when a woman gets pregnant, everybody treats her like a Goddess. There are no arguments, no fights, no shouting, no cursing. Everything is said in nice words to her and to the child in her womb. Those children are incredibly special and pure. There is no violence, and the children stay in their heart as adults because they grew up in a clean environment. The modern world today has gone into darkness. Nobody cares about anyone anymore, not even their closest ones.

We put older people into nursing homes so that we can make more money and so that we can have our own privacy. Believe me, I thought like that too Before my second trip to Colombia I was on plant medicine, Ayahuasca where I was blessed by Taita William Palchucan. There, I recognised the beauty of unity and the respect towards older and wiser people. People gather wisdom throughout their life, but of course, they are not smarter than us. We are all equally smart. Us younger people should accept the thoughts and opinions of older people even though it is not mandatory to do so. It all depends on how the elders were brought up and if it is for the well-being of the entire family. I am talking about the Colombian way of life, where the elders are respected and the younger people give all that they can to worship and work, while somebody in their family takes care of the elders, but inside the family.

Before I went to Colombia, I was chasing money so that I could find happiness.

You know what I got instead?

Depression.

I had everything that money could buy but I did not have myself. It is attention-grabbing, what do you think? I am not saying that money is bad, but getting attached to that energy is undeniably not a good thing to do. We get attached to material things and we forget all our basic human values and families. Thank God that I found something like that in my life even though it took a long time and a lot of deep endurance to get to what I have now. What I can say is that I have myself and the belief in a higher guidance. I do not need that anymore. It sounds very humble, but that is the way of the life that I live. Of course, I have wishes and I would love to have material things, but I do not worry and I do not get stressed if something does not come into my life.

6.

Attachment To Material Things

What happened before?

I suffered and I mourned for material things because my mind was programmed to feel like that. So far, I have shown you my life and what it was like with my mother and my family, but I do not know if you have forgotten that my relationship with my mother was not good. I stayed with her and my grandparents. From the beginning, everything was going alright because she was mourning for my brother and father, and I was just 14 years old. As time passed, she got a job at the nearby fishery. It was a 12-hour shift. I went to the high school to become an auto-electrician, but I was planning on becoming a policeman. Back in the good old days, we joked around at how I was going to be a policeman and that my brother would be a lawyer. That joke was not at all clear to me, because my brother did not have good grades, so it would be impossible for him to be a lawyer. I wanted to show off and I wanted to become what we were all saying that I would become. I was exceptionally good at school and most of the time I was well behaved, but I had my own moments, especially in elementary school. A lot of things were happening at home that reflected through my behaviour at school. I finished the first year of high school with an incredibly good 4, and for the police academy back then, you needed to have that grade at the first term of the second year of high school. At the beginning of the second year, I lost my brother and, before the term ended, I lost my father. I do not know why, but my religion teacher concluded that I would be getting a 1, but my report was graded at 5. I got a

1 for a test because I did not study. More than half of the class got 1 and we were all angry at the teacher. It was a nightmare. We even threw chalk at him and we kept whistling. All the students in the school looked at him malevolently and they were whistling in the corridors. It was a madhouse. My close friend broke his bike, which was beside the school, out of anger.

Why so much violence? It was a time of war in Croatia. The war was already ending, but the energy was still in the air. On the other hand, Religion was an elective course, and you should be able to get a good grade no matter what and not get a bad one to ruin the average of your grades. Yes, that is how I lost my dream of police academy, because I had a negative grade. Honestly, I was terribly angry at the teacher and I hated the way he acted. Today, I am thankful to him and I know why I was not able to enrol into the police academy. I could not enrol because I would not have become what I am today.

Why? The way I see it, during service in the military, they train the mind as well, so it puts people completely into their mind and separates them from their heart, especially in Croatia. The police are extremely strict, and they punish people everywhere. It is exceedingly rare that they let someone off without a punishment. The social life was also awfully bad, and it was hard to live. The police should work for the people and not for the country. I will tell you about something that happened in Ireland before I continue.

Yes, I was in Ireland. I spent a few years there because the Croatian way of life was boring and the complete injustice that was happening there and is still happening is annoying. The government says that they are not communists anymore, but their actions say otherwise. If a political side is in the lead, and if you do not support that political party, it makes getting material things ridiculously hard. That is what I aspired for my entire life.

Back to the incident that happened in Ireland. I was walking down the road and I saw an old lady with a mobility scooter on a road crossing just before a roundabout. I saw a Garda car (Irish police) stop and turn on the lights on top of the car. They got out of the car and helped the lady across the crossing. Tears of happiness started running down my face. My Croatian mind was expecting that the lady was going to get punished for being on a motorised wheelchair. I would have been surprised if the Croatian police had done something like that. It is not their fault, it is just the way that they are trained because of the situation in Croatia, and a lot of people are disconnected from their hearts where all the love, wisdom, compassion and acceptance are.

That was how I continued my life with my mother who worked all day. When she came home, she shouted at me and told me bad things, like, "You are useless."

In all honestly, I was. I was careless. I did not clean the house. I did not study either because I had lost the will to, because of losing the police academy opportunity. Back then I started hating her even more. You need to understand that back then I was not the same person that I am today. I understand that it is not okay to hate your parents, but that was how I felt back then.

That was how my days passed. Every night, there were fights and arguments. Today, I understand that I was often like that after I started working, and that while working, a lot of stress is built up and then all that stress is taken out on your loved ones. It is not the right way, but that was how it was.

Today, I know a lot of techniques, such as breathing exercises, that can help with stress and I also know about natural remedies from the Amazon rainforest. Those things happen because people do what they love instead of looking for a profit. It all happens because the school system is created that way, or at least it is in Croatia. We all have something that we are creatively good at. Nobody is smarter than anyone else. We are all smart in our own way. I will give you an example.

A man who went to the best colleges may not know how to change the wheel of a car, but someone who did not go to school at all may know how to do it. It all depends on what we focus our creative energy into. I started working when I was 15 years old in the same place as my mother. I cut grass with a strimmer, and I minded and fed the fish. Yes, I also went to school, but during school breaks, I worked because my mother did not want to give me money to go to the seaside with my girlfriend. Yes, when I was 15, I had a girlfriend who I had sex with and I fell in love with her. In all honesty, she was not even a good girlfriend, but she was good for a start. She used me as much as she could, a lot of other people did too, because I was a nice person and I loved to give to people. I was a target for that kind of people. My grandmother kept warning me, but I could not help myself.

Today, I can see that I was buying friendship from others just to be accepted. I was frequently rejected, and it makes sense, right? Do you see how patterns are put together and they make sense?

I can see it clearly and I can say that they are all lessons today. Lessons for me to learn to say "no", no matter what. It is the hardest thing to do, but if you feel that you have to say "no", then say it no matter what your mind says. If you do not, for me, everything starts going downhill. I will explain why.

If we give too much and we do not receive anything in return, there is an imbalance in the relationship. Imagine it as an old weighing scale with a counterweight.

A lot of the times, things happened to me when I lost those people from my life, but do you know in which way?

I was blamed for something that I did not do. Why? I would say that that sort of people subconsciously feel like they owe you, so to feel better, they blame you and give their responsibility to you. I honestly forgave every single one of them, because I live by the words that were cut into me from the Catholic church: "As we too forgive our debtors."

In a way, they were good times, and it is as if I got used to my mother's behaviour. I simply wrote her off. A few months after my father died, my mother met this hunter who was called Vojko. He is my stepfather today. I knew that something had happened that day because she gave me money to go out. That was not her usual behaviour. I knew that she wanted to get rid of me, but going out was a good idea. I took the money and went out. I felt extremely jealous and I had a bad feeling. I did not like it at all, especially with her hiding things from me as if I was an idiot.

Meanwhile, they stopped seeing each other. I knew that because I lived in a small village where everybody knew everything. My grandmother was in Germany. She had a friend called Herbert. I loved that man. He took me out every time that he was in Croatia and he bought me everything that I wanted. He drove me in his car, he was a generous person. I think it was because he was lonely. His wife had left him after she had used him good, so you see the similarities with me. I imagined a life in Germany and that my life was finally going to get better and that I would be rich.

Why?

There was a friend who was in my class in school, and his mother married a German man and they went to Germany. After a few years, when he was young, he had a lot of things and he worked with his stepfather. I thought to myself that I will finally be rich after living so poor that I could not afford a bathroom in the house. I was terribly ashamed of that fact, whenever I had friends over. They all had bathrooms, toilets and plumbing, and I had nothing. It was hard to live and wash myself in a plastic container. That was why I was always untidy and had greasy hair. I loved it when I went somewhere and they offered me the use of their bathroom. I used to spend up to an hour in the shower or in the bathtub.

Then, what happened? Something started with my mother and Herbert, but it suddenly stopped. I was in total shock and disbelief. Life was turning its back on me again. There would be nothing from Germany and no better life. My mother said that he did not suit her and that he was not good enough for her.

Today, I see why. My mother lives an old-fashioned life where the man is in charge. A lot of women think like that today. A lot of girls go for rich people who behave arrogantly, and they completely ignore the good and kind men. It is sad when they get the rich men and then they learn that it is not so easy even though they were attracted to that energy.

Why is this happening?

I think it is because women look for a man with the character traits of their fathers and, of course, subconsciously they do find them, but later in life they do not get love, they get suffering. When it is too late, that is when they consider a divorce. Believe me that is not the way things are solved. We can all succeed in marriage, but we need a lot of self-discipline and openness to change things and to talk with the other side, or to be more exact, with your partner.

Let us not forget our responsibility for our lives. It is easy to point fingers at somebody else and blame them. We can find things out about ourselves and then we can see what we can do to change things. Believe me, it is easy to keep quiet and keep everything inside of you, but after a while, all of it will come out onto your partner. Things change in the very beginning with honest conversations. In a way, this does not suit us, as we are not used to it.

"Why are you doing that?" could be replaced with

"Honestly, I'm not comfortable and I feel hurt when you do that, so can you please do it differently the next time."

Do you see the difference?

Believe me, I know what I am saying because I have been married to a woman for over 17 years. Everything is possible and it is much easier if you work with alternative methods of deep healing. Theta Healing helped me a lot and Ayahuasca helped me later. I will talk more about it later.

So that is how my mother continued her relationship with Vojko. I could not say much against her decision, even though I was asking myself whether she could have stayed with Herbert and gone to Germany just to make my life better. Later, she could have ended things. Now, I know that it is a brave thing to do, to just go somewhere unknown with nothing but a suitcase. Do you see how life is showing us things? We just need to observe what happens and use our logical mind to analyse everything.

Forgive me, I have not mentioned one vitally important thing which happened during my 17th birthday celebration. I would ask you not to judge me or my mother. You need to understand that my mind was very polluted in many ways.

My mind is not like that today.

People who have been through big changes will understand what I mean. It is necessary for you to understand that I grew up in a family full of dark energies. Later, I will explain why.

The people in my family drank alcohol. My grandfather was a serious alcoholic, who nearly went crazy because of it before he stopped. My father often drank, and he would come home with other people and even more drinking would happen. During winter, they used to play cards a lot and they drank a lot while playing. What do you think a young, uncorrupted mind would start acting like when it witnesses all those men behaving like that around it?

Even today, people think that it is "cool" to get drunk, then spend the next day talking about how drunk they got and all the crazy things they did. I will say that now I do not drink alcohol, because I learnt that that energy is directly connected to demonic energies. If a man is drunk, especially from strong alcohol, our energetic field, also known as our aura, falls away and that way various demons can attach to us. It all depends on what kind of demons we carry in us, or to be more correct, what kind of thought patterns we have. It is not an accident that people call alcohol "spirits". That ghost is not good for us in general. It is not the same if you remember some movie programmes, you think that most rich people drink whisky or some other stronger alcohol. It is not an accident that they are trying to poison your mind and the minds of your children.

"Let go of
attachments to
the material
world,
this way you are
becoming free
and abundance
is coming in your
life."

7.

Honest Life Brings Happiness

This is the part of the story where I will talk about one of the worst things I have done in my life. The second thing was when I was little, around four or five years old, when I would look around the house to find out what was there.

You know what I found?

Porno magazines under the bed where my parents slept. I often looked at them because I would never have seen anything like that in my area of the house. Everyone was hidden away wearing clothes. I even had an erection, but I did not do anything with it. To me, when I was little, that area was forbidden, unexplored, not discussed. I used to hide in case anyone found out that I looked at them. I did not know that it darkened and poisoned my mind, as I was too little to understand. My parents were hiding sex from my brother and me, which was not healthy at all.

Today, I know that because it brings more harm than good. I heard my parents do it a few times, but I cannot say that I ever saw them do it.

Why is it not good?

I had a treatment session with this one boy, who had difficult problems with sex, or to be more exact, he did not really enjoy sex with his girlfriend. Do you know what we ended up finding in his subconscious? When he was around six years old, he caught his parents having sex. To him, it was a big trauma, because he thought that his father was hurting his mother, as she was making loud noises. You see how hiding things makes them worse than when we are honest with our children. During treatment, I intuitively got insights that my son had seen me and my wife having sex, and I regretted not explaining it to him. So, when I came home, I talked with him. He was nine or ten years old. I asked him if he had ever seen us, and he said that he had. I then explained to him that it is a completely normal thing to do when you love someone and that we would not hide it. Instead, we would rather be open and honest with him, and ask him to go outside and play when we want to be together.

Do you see how today's society is based on shame? This is one of the lower vibrations compared to love and honesty. That is why I am inviting you to be honest with one another and to be honest with your children. Forget what you were taught and make the changes that you want to see in this world. If something ever bothers you about someone, I can guarantee you that it is something in you and yours. It is something that you are unaware of doing or were unaware of being.

My mind was corrupted with sexual things. I had a lot of encounters with girls. I even stayed over, sleeping with a girl in the same bed. I do not know how, but we both ended up naked and having sex. I played a game with a girl where we took our clothes off and looked at each other. We called it observing. We would get naked somewhere where nobody would see us and we would observe each other's bodies. It was just looking, not touching. After the girl started puberty, she did not want to do it anymore because she started getting shy.

There was quite a difficult situation when I got my brother, who was only four at the time, to ask our neighbour's daughter, who was the same age as him, to have sex with us. The game was that I would pretend to drive the car wreck that was in our orchard behind the house and my brother would try to have sex with her. Then we would change places and I would try. We did but with no success. After a few days of doing that, the girl got bored and she told her mother. I did not know where to hide from the shame and, honestly, I do not know where I got all those ideas from. I just maybe wanted to study and practise sex because I was surrounded by that kind of energy.

Today, I am deeply sorry for what I did, but I cannot turn back time. I can however be honest and share my truths with you. I hope that you still see me as a normal person, but you should know that my mindset was much different back then than it is now. Unfortunately, that is not the end of the things that I have done, and I will continue telling my truths no matter what the consequences.

Believe me, this book is like a confession to God. Only through the truth can we come to the God inside of us.

I celebrated my 15th birthday. The fact that my brother and father had died made my mother act softer because she let me celebrate my birthday in the house. Of course, there was alcohol, a lot of it. My peers came from the capital, Zagreb. We all drank a lot, and I invited my older girlfriend there too. I do not know why I did not have sex with her. I felt awkward asking, so we just stayed kissing. She went home and we all continued drinking. We were all very drunk. Now, I am asking you not to judge my mother because she was lost too. She just wanted to make me feel better because

I used to come home drunk a lot. She could not change me. I knew that she knew that the deaths we had witnessed bothered me a lot.

Later that the night, a girl came over and she was also visibly drunk. We drank on with the rest of the people in the house. I walked her out because I think that she wanted to go to the toilet. When she was done, something inside of me, I think most probably demons, started acting out. I started touching her and I wanted to have sex with her. Because she was drunk, she did not put up much resistance. The house was empty, so we were alone. I do not remember how we ended up in my room, where I started taking her clothes off. Unfortunately, she did not want me to, but I continued anyway. Forgive me for writing this, believe me, it is not easy for me to write it. I keep thinking I should take this out of the book, but no, I will not because my heart wants to speak the truth.

Her being drunk was how I managed to take off her clothes. I had forced sex with her. I stripped her quickly, and when the sex started, she stopped trying to move away. She lay there and she let me do it. Afterwards, I helped her get dressed and I walked her home. The next day I was panicking because I thought I was going to end up in jail. I think that I needed to, because it is something that I am not proud of in my life. Then again, I am saying that this body was suffering with dark energies which were guiding my life. The third day I met her, and I was afraid of what she was going to say, but she just asked me what had happened, saying that she had forgotten everything. I told her that nothing had happened, out of fear.

Yes, I lied. I knew I should not have done so. That situation was forgotten until I eventually began the process of healing myself. During the treatment, I felt every bit of pain and trauma that I inflicted on the girl. Believe me, I hated myself and my actions. I felt enormous pain and suffering, and I could not snap myself back for about an hour. I drove home in tears. It was around 70km away from where I was having the treatment.

In this way, whoever I hurt in my life, I have been given the opportunity to say that I hope that they can find the strength to forgive me for all that I have done to them. I also hope that you too (girl that I abused) forgive me, the same way that I have forgiven a lot of people in my life who have browbeaten me. You should know that after the treatment, I felt so down that I was thinking of killing myself because of the harm that I had done to that girl. On the way home from Zagreb, I asked for help from my friend, who dug into my subconscious and made me forgive myself totally, because I felt like I was her and that she was me.

Once again, I am sorry.

Yes, I have lived through rape attempts too, but not from women, from men. I know that a lot of people thought that I was gay, but I was not. I had a mental disorder towards genders in my thoughts. I even tried to masturbate thinking about men, but deep inside, I was attracted to women. I know that three things affected my sexuality. The first was my childhood, which was full of punishments and the extraction of the male energy out of me. The second was my mother and her wish to have a girl, and the third was that my mother went to check my temperature once and she could not put the thermometer under my armpit or my mouth so, she forcefully pushed the thermometer into my backside.

I know that my mother was not aware of what her actions did to me, but for me, it was a massive trauma. I had so many big traumas that I could write ten more books if I remembered everything. Honestly, today, I do not remember everything as much as I did before. That is why it is so hard for me to write, because my memories are coming back as I write this book. You will see later that it is not all so black and white in my life, even though I spent more than 30 years in darkness.

Let me get back to my experiences.

The first one was when I was 13. When I was getting my Christian rite, I got a bicycle from my godfather. I was at the local tavern and we were drinking beers. Yes, I drank then too, but not as much. I was there with a friend. Some old man offered me 20 kunas if I would give him a lift home on my bike. For me, this was easy money, as it was more than I would get at home. The man was very drunk, and he sat on the seat. I cycled for around 400 metres. It was dark, but I had a light on the bike. The man then started touching me under my shirt. For around 200 metres, he kept touching me. I was scared but I kept quiet. I was looking for a way to get away. We came to a hill and I told him to get down because I did not have the strength to go on. He got off and I cycled away as fast as I could. After that, I would see him around, but he never said anything and neither did I.

I forgave him and I even felt sorry for him because he lived alone with his father and his life was not the best.

The second time something happened to me was when I was serving in the military. I went down a path of drugs and alcohol at the time, but I will talk more about that later. I was on duty in my building. I had a visitor, so I drank two beers with my friend and even took ecstasy. It was an interesting night and there was a lot of banter. Some boys had some weed, so I smoked some of that as well. I was completely out of myself. I fell asleep in the entrance where I was supposed to be on duty. The barracks officer came and shouted at me, but he could not wake me up. He went into the sentry box to tell a soldier to come and get me. He woke me up first try. I do not remember how I woke up or anything. We went to the sentry box and I was sober as if nothing had happened. That was where the barracks officer was waiting for me with a gloomy look on his face. He asked me where I was and I answered. He shouted at me and asked me why I was asleep and why he could not wake me up. I had to lie because the punishments were extremely harsh in the military. I said that I did not remember and that I had not heard him at all, and that when the soldier came for me, I had heard him straight away, which the soldier confirmed. He was surprised by the situation and he said that we were going to talk in my building.

On the way there, he asked me to answer him honestly if I had consumed something and I said yes that I had drunk two beers and that as I was not used to it, I fell asleep. He had calmed down as we entered the building, we sat down and watched TV and talked. Suddenly, he put his arm on my shoulder. I was scared. Thousands of thoughts were going through my head on how to escape. I was afraid of getting punished and getting shouted at by him if I say something wrong. I was lucky. I decided to lean on the table as if nothing happened. He noticed that I did not want anything to do with him and he decided to leave. I was so happy. First, he caught me sleeping and then I was almost raped. I know that he was sober at the time, but a lot could have happened if he was drunk.

As you can see, I did not feel too comfortable even though nobody forced me into sex, but there were attempts.

Now, I can say that after I had healed that part of myself, a few female clients who were raped, even in their families, came to me for help. I had full compassion for the victim and a deeper understanding of the rapist. I would have loved to learn it in a different way, but my soul decided to teach me the hardest way. There were other things connected to karma, and it is very possible that that was being done.

Life is extremely complicated, and it is not easy to understand how it works. Today, I know that our feelings and our sober being tell us whatever we need to know. A lot of people suffer because they want to run away from their feelings. A lot of people are also depressed and anxious. I will tell you now that everything is okay with you, but it is necessary for you to find out why you are depressed and what is the cause of your anxiety, or to be more exact, your deep fear.

Depression is a sign that you have supressed yourself and that you do not live your life the way you should. For example, no matter what you do and no matter how much money it gives you, it still does not make you happy. Depression and anxiety are very easily solved with the healing methods that I do today.

I honestly hope that I have not shocked you with my truths and that you have continued reading. The ending will not be so dark. Instead, it is going to be incredibly positive. All that I have written is to show you that no matter what you are like or what you were like, it is possible to heal and change. You just need to wish for it and be persistent with your intentions.

I will go back to my life with my mother. She had secretly started a relationship with Vojko, who I did not like that much, mostly because she was not honest with me. From my point of view, she lied to me, treating me like I was stupid. That lasted for some time. I finished high school, which I chose to do, because there was not a lot of subjects to study so that I could join the police academy. That fell apart and so did my life as an auto-electrician. Why? At the time, there were not many private auto-electricians who I could be an apprentice to, so I just went to a company where my father used to work called Čazmatrans. That is where I learnt a decent number of things, but the auto-electricians did not like me. They treated me like scum, and so that was what I started to become. I was never bad towards them, but they treated me badly, just like the most of my family.

Do you notice a pattern?

Later at work, I got closer to an orthodox mechanic. Croatia was still at war against the Serbs and the Serbs were orthodox. I did not care who was what, because a person is a person, no matter what they are or what they look like. I believe that he had a similar case of not belonging as I did, so he accepted me to learn from him. With him, I learnt more in one year than I learnt with any of the others in two years. Thank you, Nedeljko.

My mother continued with her behaviour and she often threatened me with words.

"You're a piece of shit and you're worthless, and I will leave you."

I was already used to her acting like that, and I honestly did not even care anymore. I even thought that it would be a good thing if she left me.

"I will be alone and independent," I thought to myself at the time.

I was young then, only around 17 years old. That spring of 1999, my mother took in her brother Renato to live with us in the house. Renato was an awfully bad person. He stole, drank and took drugs. He did not have his own house, so he moved around from house to house. Renato helped her to de-kernel corn off the cobs, and my mother did not want me anywhere near her again. I did not know what was happening. She was mad at me and often told me that she was leaving. When they were finished with the corn, she took it and sold it, and then she gave some money to Renato but none to me. She told me that I did not deserve anything and that she was leaving the house, and that I should figure out how to live on my own. Now, I will ask you another thing. What would you think if your own mother kept repeating that you are worthless and that you are a piece of shit? What would you be like?

She used those words when I was younger too. I will tell you now that those types of words and that sort of behaviour affects the mentality, and so you should try not to use those kinds of words towards your children. If you cannot lift someone up, then do not put them down. So, my mother left me to be with my uncle when I was a little bit older than 17.

I stayed in the house with my grandparents. My grandfather did not care much for me, but my grandmother promised me that she would help me as much as she could. She did not have a particularly good pension and she was extremely sick, so she spent most of her money on medicines and doctors. My grandfather had an even smaller pension and a few farm animals that took more than they gave back. My grandfather did not see it or did not want to see it. I believe that he had them so that he had something to do and so that he had to move around and keep active. In our village, people say that you are worthy if you work a lot. I will ask you all now, does hard work make a man worthy or is it his stability that makes him worthy no matter what he is like? I would say that we are all of equal value because we are people, and that way we are a part of God so that makes us all equal. Those were old beliefs in Croatia that are slowly being replaced, just like the old way of life. The new ways of life have separated us from our neighbours and families.

Why?

There were never a lot of machines back in the day, so everyone went around and helped each other. Well, there were families who were like that. Most who were like that were our cousins and godparents. Nobody asked who had more or who had less. Everyone helped each other no matter what. Today, everyone has machines, and they work alone. Before, we used to go visit each other, especially during the winter times when there was less work to do, and in the summer during the highest temperatures, we would sit in the shade and tell stories, and unfortunately talk behind people's backs. Today, nobody has time because they work all the time just to earn as much as they can so that they can have as many material things as possible. It is not bad to own material things, but to be attached and to waste your precious life just working for material things is not a particularly good option. We are here to enjoy life and not to suffer, which is what a lot of people think is normal.

I would say that the Christian church has a big role to play in all of that with programming people into thinking that they should suffer just like Jesus suffered. I will tell you now that if you want to be close to God, you must learn some basic human values, such as unconditional giving, compassion, honesty, love, respect and forgiveness. Unconditional giving is the hardest of all the things to learn. A lot of people say today that they give things to each other. A lot of people give because they expect something back, something that they want and not something that is given. That is not unconditional, that is planned. God does not work that way. Every day, God gives us things unconditionally. We just need to learn to accept them and to give in the same way, because then we are at one with God.

Over the years, I have learnt how to give and to accept in that way, and today I know how to give unconditionally and how to accept things that are given unconditionally if the Creator wants it that way. I am not attached to profit, money or anything material things that I own. I have things, but I do not worry if I get more. Interesting, isn't it? If you are being led by low vibrations such as shame, jealousy, envy, hatred and resentment, you should know that you are distancing yourself from God. If someone has wealth, they can have more of it. We all see material things when they are there, but we never question the way that someone got to them. In Croatia, a lot of people got their wealth in an unfair way, but you should know that justice does exist and it is not up to us to judge people. There is a law of cause and effect, and the people who earn things unfairly will suffer the consequences of their dishonesty.

Remember my great grandfather and all the things that he had done. He did a lot of bad things and that is why we had a karmic life. It is all a part of a big divine plan so that we can see each other with our hearts and, with our love, we can remember who we are and where we are going. We are all going towards the Creator, and I will be brave and say that what it says in the Bible about the dead rising just means that people will start awakening just the way that I did. A dead person is a person who acts like a zombie and who lives in their mind and not in their heart. That is what Jesus is trying to show you in images of him holding a finger on one hand towards his heart and pointing three fingers on the other hand towards the sky. You should know that I am no longer Catholic, but Jesus is still in my heart and I respect him as one of the best teachers who lived on Earth to show us the way to our hearts and how to be more truthful to God. Our heart is scientifically proven to be the centre of everything that happens in our bodies. It is up to us to connect to that centre and to live our lives in our hearts together with the mind.

Back to my mother leaving me. I lived with my uncle for a while. I managed to find a proper job. My uncle worked at a builder in the village, and I got a job at a different builder. I was 64kg, around 170cm tall, and I was skinny and small. The work that I did was so hard that, in the mornings, I could hardly walk to the place where I would get picked up to go to work. I worked hard for three days and I know that I did not satisfy the owner of the company. I was open and ready to do whatever he wanted me to do, but he turned his back on me. It was not easy, but at least, I earned myself some money so that I could live. After that, I did not work much. Instead, we just had parties in my house. My uncle was acting badly, and he stole the gold that I earned as a gift, so I kicked him out of the house. I stayed with my grandparents. In those years, I had a lot of freedom, which led me to my demise.

I smoked cigarettes, drank alcohol and encountered marijuana. When I go back to that time, everything was great. I was enjoying things, I had total freedom and there was banter with good company every night. That could not last long though because I did not have a job. So, I found another job, which was often harder than the first one. I started working in the fishery where they grew consumer fish. It was a torturous job, but it gave me money so that I could live normally. Unfortunately, nobody taught me how to save money or how to use it properly, so I spent all my money on clothes, alcohol and drugs. It is the sad truth, but now that I think about it, if it were any different, I would not be the way I am today. It was all going well until winter came. There was no work for around three months, and I had no money. My grandmother did not have much either because she spent most of her money on doctors. She went to dialysis for her kidneys. Her kidneys were in an awfully bad state.

She often said that pro-fascist collaborators had done that to her. She was naked and, in all probability, raped in jail. She slept on naked concrete. Today, I know that it is very possible, but not because she was sleeping on concrete but because she resented them. If you have problems with your kidneys, those sorts of organs gather energies of hate and resentment towards others. I remember that winter like it was yesterday because I had thought so many times about killing myself. I was depressed, lonely and rejected by my mother, who did not give me anything. My grandmother comforted me, and she was a huge support to me. If it were not for her and for her love, I would have killed myself by now. I did not know better back then, and I was not taught that we create life, and I do not remember how or when things would become better. I think that my grandmother lent me money so that I could buy cigarettes. That spring I started working. Unfortunately, I did not change, and I forgot about that winter. I was planning on buying myself a car so that I would have something to drive around in. "No car, no girls", I thought to myself. I asked the owner of the company where I worked at if I could get paid in advance and that I would work for free, and he accepted my offer. My grandmother helped me with her small pension so that I could get a driver's licence. She was the miracle in my life.

I bought my first car and the world felt like it was mine. I did not consider the car to be an expense and I did not even think of the next winter, I was just going out. Going out and enjoying myself with friends, drugs and alcohol. Yes, unfortunately, I lived like that, in the dark and separated from the light which I carried in me and which you all carry in you. The days passed and I thought about better pay even though I spent everything that I earned. Of course, I did not always get it and the time came when I did.

As my relationship with my mother was not good, I decided to calm down when she gave birth to my half-brother, Saša. For some reason, I was happy, and I decided to contact them. I went to visit my half-brother and my mother. He was unbelievably cute, especially because he had blonde hair like Nino. I started liking him and I saw in him that which I had lost. After a while, my stepfather became good friends with a wealthy man who owned a concrete plant. I was a good worker, so they helped me get a job there, where the pay was almost double what I used to get where I worked before. The only problem was that I had to live there and not with my grandparents. I was going to "earn the bread" (Croatian Proverb) as if I were hungry, as people in my village say. I had a vision that I would buy a better car, that I would save money and that I would be rich. I left out the most important part.

I did not change and all the behaviour with alcohol and drugs got worse. I ploughed deeper into the world of darkness. I got an even better car, but it was a wreck that my stepfather had. It looked good on the outside, but it was a bit rusty. I think I paid too much for it, but it was a good deal with the owner of the plant and my stepfather. The owner gave money to my stepfather and I worked on the car. I had enough money back then but I did not save anything. I spent most of it on going out and drugs. I was a hard worker there, and while the other workers had proper lives, I did not.

I asked myself how can they have good lives and not me?

I will tell you how. If you look back at my past and the way that I lived, you can see that I did not have anyone to teach me how to live because my past was hospitals, alcohol, and often arguments and punishments. You can see now what can happen to your children if you are constantly having arguments in the family. I do not know if you know, but when parents argue, the children feel guilty. They carry that guilt and feel rejected, which later leads the children to subconsciously destroy their lives and to have mental issues, such as depression or anxiety. All diseases are psychological, and they come from the mind and the way that we are programmed and taught to live. So, I had an enormous income, but I was always broke. I even asked my grandmother if I could "borrow" some money so that I could have money for food because I had spent all the money I'd earned in a single weekend.

We got weekly pay, and I always spent the maximum every time.

"Live your life in your unique way without following others and acting like them. Other people can be an example to you, but you should extract only the best things to find your own uniqueness."

8.

Ego Mind

So, the time to join the military came. I did not want to go. I did not want to lose my freedom, but I had to go. Today, I am grateful for that experience because I had let myself go. I was not tidy or clean. It was like that after the military, but something cracked in me later. It was as if something was inside of me. There was something in me, something that always corrected my life. I thought it was a punishment, but it was the Creator. He guided me from difficult situations and was showing me that something was wrong. My mind has persistently rejected listening to it and I went deeper into the world of drugs, with a constant consumption of ecstasy and weed followed by alcohol and smoking. A lot of people would say that it was a great life. I found myself doing that because I had "friends" and they accepted me for being like that. Today, I know that that was not a good decision, but time cannot be reversed.

I learnt a different type of discipline in the military, where the ego had to be low and there was no right of speech. I learnt what tidiness meant and how to take care of myself. After the military, even though I still enjoyed drugs and alcohol on the weekends, I started to learn how to cook and how to make cakes for the holidays. My friends, at least I thought they were my friends, made fun of me and I intuitively knew that they thought that I was gay because I was doing "women jobs".

You should know that my grandmother was not well, and neither was my grandfather. Slowly despite the drugs, I started to turn around towards my creative side and towards a home life. That is the natural survival instinct, because I knew that my grandparents would not live long.

In the military, I was also punished, so that shook me a bit more. They caught me with some weed and I ended up in detention. Somehow, the worst thing for me was that I lost my freedom, and it was one of the worst days in my life. After returning from the military, I hoped to start working in the place where I used to work. Nothing went to plan, because in the meantime, I had crashed the car and I did not have the money for a new one.

It is the same as I am saying today, weed held me back. I did not want to do anything. I forgot a lot, was untidy and nobody could rely on me. That was not my true nature. That was why, one time, I promised a worker where I worked ensiling corn that I would help him, but I did not help him, I stayed home and smoked weed.

Later, after returning home from the military, I asked him if I could work with them because I knew that they had a free space in the car, but he rejected me in a nice way by saying that they did not have any space in the car. The lie and rejection hurt me. That was when I started learning from my mistakes. I understood how much my smoking weed and not helping was costing me.

Everything happens for a reason and it is up to us to observe the world around us. If you want a good life, then you should act unselfishly towards others. That was when I started to learn in life that I was not a saint. I started thinking more, even though I was preoccupied with alcohol and weed. I stopped taking ecstasy and I noticed that there was a giant leap in my awareness after I stopped taking it. Somehow, my existence felt much better and my character was stronger.

Though I did not know what our ego mind is for in life, to be more correct, it is selfish behaviour. Ego mind is good and it keeps us connected to this world, but we often get tied into its influence and end up in pain and suffering. The ego mind plans and wants to be the best in the world, the richest, the most famous, the strongest, the most beautiful, but the heart wants to just be and enjoy observing the world. I would not say that I was in the heart back then, but I still studied people and their patterns of behaviour.

There were a lot of topics around these things with the people with whom I spent time. I realised that all the people who accepted me when I took ecstasy were in their ego mind and they were fake. Everything they did was fake. We acted "cool", but we were rotten on the inside. That is why it is important who we are on the inside and not on the outside. Today, a lot of people buy clothes, make-up, cars, houses and so on, so that they can show to the world how good they look and that they are hard-working and that they are wealthy. Believe me, the biggest wealth is when a person knows themself and is at peace with it. You cannot buy that kind of wealth, but you can create it. That is one of the reasons why I am writing this book, to inspire you in a way that you can see that someone who has had a hard life and did awfully bad things has made a change. I would even say that that was my life goal. That is why today the respect of a person is worth most to me. Everything else for me has no value.

This may be hard to understand, but if you start going along the path of your heart, you will understand what I am talking about. And that was how I lost a well-paid job.

I did not give up on life and my job. I believed that I would find work somewhere because I was a hard-working person and a good worker. Everybody praised me, but they objected to the fact that I fell asleep at work. As I often took drugs, I did not hear the alarm go off. That was what it was like for me, and you see how much it damaged me. In fact, it did damage me because I felt ashamed and not good enough. I was not surprised that I created those kinds of situations when during my whole life everyone told me that I was worthless. You see how things function? I created those situations on my own where I ended up feeling like I was not good enough. Believe me, the only way you can live your life properly is in this way. Take responsibility for your life. That means no matter what situations you get into, your energy and vibration affect other people around you. If you feel that you are not enough, then other people will feel and say these things about you, and you will feel hurt. Unfortunately, many people look for someone to blame, so they blame their partners, bosses or anyone else. The world around you is your mirror. So, if you see that the world around you is not the way you want it to be, do anything you can to find an alternative form of healing to help you live more easily. All of this is extremely complicated, because you are just not yourself, you are your mother, your father and all of your ancestors who act through your DNA chain.

I've wondered off again, but I am just following the impulse from my heart and I do not think about what I write. I just let my hand do the work. I started talking about me believing in myself and that I would find work. I found it at a nearby farm at my neighbours. He was righteous and good. He gave me a chance and he helped himself too. He often said that I was too fast for him and that I should slow down. I just worked at a pace that I'd learnt, even though I listened to him and did not go too fast. It all depended on my needs and my feelings. Because the village was small, stories started spreading about how good a worker I was. Frequently, the people in the village were saying the same things as my mother, that I would never become somebody and that I was a waste of space. I did not care, and I lived my life the best way that I knew how to.

One day, the farmer started thinking and told me that he did not need a worker anymore. I knew that he had made a mistake, he even told me that later, but I accepted it. I was jobless again. One day, a miracle happened. At least, in my eyes, it was a miracle. A neighbour who had an even bigger farm offered me a job, to help him build a new building at his farm. I knew that I had to prove to him that I was a good worker and that I could do quality work. He sent me off to break concrete. I kept breaking it until lunch and when he came to get me to eat, he was pleasantly surprised. I broke more than he thought I was going to break for the entire day. That is how after a few days, he was so pleased with my work that he offered me work every day. I was so happy. My grandmother was happy. It was the first time in my life that I had worked nearby my house with no expenses. I did not have a car at the time.

"Life is progress,
always give your
maximum when
you are doing
something. Your
potential is
limitless, only
your mind is
limiting you."

9.

Gratitude For Your Life

Yet another miracle happened. That miracle was my wife, who I am still with to this day. Somehow, she helped me to be more settled. Her love changed my point of view on life. I found hope for a better life. I had looked for girls before but not none were like her. I even had a girlfriend from the city, and she wanted me to leave my grandparents. After that comment, I did not want to have any kind of relationship with her. Something cut deep into me, and I completely agreed with it, that is that younger people need to help older people when they cannot live on their own anymore. In the village, that used to be normal, but in the more modern times, people send their elders into nursing homes where their lives tend to be worse because nursing homeowners in Croatia are extremely strict. Unfortunately, it is like that there. I wish I had the power to stop those types of things from happening, because older people need to live the rest of their lives with dignity. They are the ones who built and worked for our future. The world today excludes them and sees them as a burden. They are not a burden; they are just not the way that they used to be. They are also people and, just like us, they deserve to be treated equally if not better than younger people. They carry a lot of wisdom and it is up to us to hear them.

That was when something good started happening in my life. I believe that I was smarter and I started thinking more that I wanted to have a partner, as everyone was telling me to get a partner and get married. There had been a lot of girls before, but none were like my love, Antonija. We started seeing each other more. She was poor, well her family was poor. She lived in an old house made of wood, mud and straw, and I lived in a brick house. That is what I thought back then anyway, even though it was not important to me what she had. It was important to me that she was nice towards me and that she listened to me, which is what people in the past taught me to look for in a girl. The only problem for us seeing each other was a car. I had to beg others to go pick her up and drop her back the next day, as she was young and her parents only allowed her to stay just one night. In the end, the brother of Dražen who hired me, Mirko was his name, drove me once and he told me that we needed to do something so that they could help me buy a car.

That all happened after I lost the most valuable person in my life.

I wandered off with my thoughts and forgot that my grandmother died before I got a car. Yes, unfortunately after Antonija came over a few times, my grandmother's condition got worse, and it looked as if she was going to die. I was not ready for another loss. I often prayed for her and for God not to take her. She always helped me, and she raised me and loved me the most. She used to say that after I got married then she could die. That was how it was, except I had not married. However, I had the women I love by my side. Today, I believe that my grandmother thought that Antonija was the right woman for me, and so she let go of her heavy life full of pain. This time, I had a chance to say goodbye to her properly. I told her everything that was in my heart. I even asked her if my grandfather Josip was my real grandfather. She said that it was the truth. People always said that he was not my real grandfather, but he really was. Josip was my real grandfather, who I called Dada (YesYes on Croatian) when I was younger. Do you understand the significance? I told you before that the Creator was showing me the truth and my grandmother confirmed that. I asked for her to come to me in any way possible to confirm that she was okay. She accepted this and promised me that she would come. I am writing this in tears because I remember the pain of my loss and what happened the next year. My grandmother died at the end of November and she was buried on Nino's birthday, on the 2nd of December 2002, and that was completely unexpected. I think that it was God's plan to show me all the signs he was showing me.

What my grandmother promised me she did early in the morning on the 14th of February 2003. It was a day of love. In the morning when I was sleeping, she was in my dreams. Believe it or not, it was real. She hugged me without saying a word. I am stopping to write because of the tears whilst remembering it. You do not need to believe me, but for me, the feeling that she came and that she had kept her promise that she would be with me was 100% real. Today, I know that for a fact. Of course, it is not her body that is with me, it is her energy. Everything is energy and this world is not as material as it seems. A lot of scientific research proves this. This is an electric Universe, and we are electromagnetic beings. I questioned that a lot until I went to see the amount of minerals and vitamins in the body. Imagine this. They did not take any blood, they just connected electrodes to my face and that was how they got my mineral and vitamin count. We also know that all impulses going from our brain to the rest of our bodies are electromagnetic. Where is the battery then? Deep down, I know that we are powered by our crown chakra and we get energy from it, especially when we sleep and when we eat, even though there are people who do not eat at all and they are called breatharians.

There is a method of looking at the sun where our batteries are being charged. That is why we live in the illusion and our mind receives electric impulses from the environment and creates pictures in the centre of our mind located in the rear of our brains. This way we can see the environment around us even with our eyes closed. It is only existence or consciousness.

Why do we suffer then?

I believe that we are in a new age where people understand more and that they are awakening from their dreams. I believe that suffering in this world will stop over the next few years. I talked about why people suffer, so I will not repeat myself. I can tell you that you should find the path to your heart so that you can stop the suffering created from your mind. That is just your decision.

My grandmother ended up dying right in front of my eyes. Her life started slowly shutting down after I managed to say goodbye properly. It was exceedingly difficult. Firstly, I lost her, and, secondly, everything that I'd managed to save up, I spent on her funeral. I even stayed in debt because my grandfather did not have enough money.

Have you noticed the difference?

I even started saving back then and I lived life on a minimum wage. You can see that I was slowly starting to change. I had the thought that I wanted to create something in my life and that I wanted to prove to this world that I was not worthless. Antonija started coming over more often after my grandmother's death. She even stayed for a few days at a time. If she had not been there for me, I think that I would have killed myself because I could not handle my grandmother's death.

The next year in February, I bought a better car and Antonija moved in with me. We started to live together and, from the beginning, it was wonderful. We were not properly raised, so we learnt from our mistakes. Because I worked ten-hour shifts and I only had Sundays off, I wanted to spend some time with Antonija. Every morning, she would make it hard for me to go to work with words like "Don't go". I did not want to go, but I had to. It was a hard winter after my grandmother died and because we spent all my money on my grandmother's funeral, and I did not prepare any wood for the winter. It was very cold in the house and we honestly had nothing to eat for a few days. The fridge was empty, and we had no money. I had to borrow money just so that we could live normally.

All of these were lessons where I learnt from my mistakes. Because I worked for the richest people in the village, I started to pick up their behaviour. I then understood that if I worked hard like they did, I would be able to create something with my life. I can say that they helped me a lot with their advice.

Let us go back to Antonija and our life together. I grew up in a hard environment and I had a lot of supressed anger, so arguments started to pop up. We did not argue a lot in the beginning, but she was a little bit wild and I was not a saint. The tradition in Croatia is that the woman must listen to the man, and that he is the head of the house. After arguments, she would storm out of the room and slam the doors. That reminded me of the time when my parents broke the door, because they had arguments and they slammed the doors too.

I warned her with a calm voice a few times, but she did not listen. Then suddenly, I lashed out with all my anger. I did not want to do it, but there was a lot of supressed dark energies in me, so I did. We were arguing and she slammed the door again. This time, she went inside because she was standing in the entrance to the living room. My hand went of its own accord and I slapped her so hard that she fell onto the couch in the living room. I regretted it instantly and I felt guilty and remorseful. I apologised to her and I told her that I was sorry. Remember that I was abused, and I saw lots of people get abused. That is how my mind was programmed and I was not even aware that I did that.

Unfortunately, that was the beginning of everything. Antonija loved me with all her heart, and I loved her too. Every two to three weeks, we had an argument of some kind like that. I could not help myself because I was under a lot of stress. I regretted everything bad that I did to my loved one. I was looking for a solution, so I went to the local doctor and told her in confidence about what had been happening and I looked to her for help. That was when I encountered tranquiliser tablets. After I drank a dose, I did not function normally. I lost myself. It was worse than any drug. I did not want to take any of that ever again. Knowing that if I did not take it, I would continue the abuse to my family, it was hard, honestly. Every time that something happened, I was like a timebomb that you could not touch.

Dear Antonija, this is the way I want to thank you for the strength and love and forgiveness that you gave me when you suffered all those bad moments with me. I am sorry. I love you. Forgive me, please!

To people who are reading this, please forgive me for this too. I hope that you know that a completely different person is writing this book now, a person who has managed to heal himself with the wish to become a better person.

I am thankful to the enormous love from Antonija towards me. Her life was not easy either. Her family's behaviour was almost identical to mine. Her mother drank a lot and she used to get beaten by her. Her father was very calm, but sometimes, he used to physically punish her. We lived in a time when these things were normal and there were even harsher punishments in school. I do not want to remove the responsibility from myself for my behaviour. I am writing this so that you can see the pattern in my life that kept repeating, even with Antonija.

Antonija had a brother and her father often praised him, but he would put Antonija down. He did not do it consciously, because in Croatia, a lot of male parents think that it is an honour to have a son.

Today, I am thankful to everyone and mostly to God for sending me my life companion who is a female version of me. We have a lot of similarities and a lot of differences. The differences are there so that we can find a balance in them and the similarities are there so that we can share together in love and understanding. What I can say to you now is that Antonija did not have any kind of upbringing and a lot of people tried to make me change my mind, but I did not listen to them. I listened to my heart and I believed that she could change. When she moved in, she did not do much. She did not cook or clean. She often just did what she did at home, which was watch TV. She did not know how as she had never been shown.

Luckily, we agreed on one thing, and that was that we wanted a better and richer life. We were tired of being poor and not having anything. Antonija was a great companion because she often listened to my advice and ideas that made us materially richer. If only there were no arguments, our lives would be perfect, which is true today. No matter the arguments or anything, our love existed then and it still exists today. True love is indestructible if we want to keep it in our lives. Somehow, we arrived at the conclusion that even though she was under eighteen, we wanted to start a family. Together, we decided to have children even though we were both children ourselves. I was not even 22 at the time. One month has passed with us having sex every day, and she did not get pregnant. Another month passed and she still did not get pregnant. After that, we thought that we could not have children.

We tried again and again, even though we both felt that we were not going to get our own child, a material creation made from our love. I know exactly when she got pregnant because we both wished for a child from our hearts. It was an evening when we started talking about the topic of children. We both cried because we could not have a child. At the time, a lot of people our age had children accidentally even after having sex just the once and they often got married because of it. It was quite a trend back then and we wanted one, but we could not. We cried and we tried again, and then we forgot about our wish. I continued releasing my seed into her nevertheless, just in case. The next month, her period was different, it ended sooner. We hoped that she was pregnant. We waited for the next one in hope that she was pregnant, but it did not come. Yaaaay, we had done it!

We were happy, although my behaviour ruined that happiness in our relationship. I do not know if you noticed, but the law of attraction was used there. It was a later insight. At the time, I did not know about any laws other than the ones in church. The law of attraction works in a way that we wish for something, feel an emotion as if it was real and how we would love to have it, and then release that wish and let the Creator decide. A lot of the time a dream or wish would come true later in my life.

The saddest thing about me not knowing and having an enormous amount of anger was that I continued to physically abuse Antonija during her pregnancy. We even had sex a few days before she was due because I wanted to. Unfortunately, I was unaware of what I know today about the child feeling everything its mother feels during pregnancy. I know that today I would act differently if Antonija ever got pregnant again. I would not recommend sex during pregnancy if you want to have a special child. Remember, if you want to have a special child, it is a big responsibility and it will take years for you to create it to be pure and full of love.

There may be a lot of rejection and self-control, but do not be too hard on yourself. Today, I know that everything happens for a reason. That is how my life happened. There were awfully bad scenarios, but behind everything, there was a lesson. But we only learn if we choose to see and to start to observe life in that way. Because Antonija was pregnant, and in our small Christian community, it was a disgrace to not be married and to have a child, and also because we wanted to baptise the child in the church and we couldn't unless we were married, we decided to get married.

Somehow, I managed to save up money, but not enough to have a big wedding. The local tamburitza band "Štefanjska zvona" offered to play at our wedding for free, because they felt that it was a good thing to do. I was extremely thankful, and I still am to this day.

I will never forget that day. It was peaceful even though there was a lot of alcohol. Of course, I overdid it. There was a lot of fun and partying, but in an inappropriate way from my point of view today.

Why?

Once I had insight and it was a concept that passed through my head. A person was listening to folk music that did not have any positive lyrics in it. They were all like "I drink to forget" and so on. The concept was that people were happy because of alcohol and around them were little demons, like the gremlins from the movies. I know that it is hard to understand, but my vision was my vision and a feeling. If you are reading this with your mind, it may be hard to understand, but everyone I know today says that I am authentic and honest. I do not have a reason to lie about that. So, the little demons were happy at my wedding, but of course that was not enough evil, so chaos started.

Before the end of the wedding, it is traditional for the bride to go and change their clothes. We went to my house, which was not too far from where we celebrated. We took the gifts that we got with the help of our godparents. We were excited to see how much money we got as a gift. We were in debt because of the wedding, and we needed some money for ourselves for our life. Antonija counted the money that I got from my best man. It was as much money as my monthly pay. That was a lot for me at the time and it seemed like a big responsibility at the time, and even today it is still a lot of money.

I wanted to take the money from where we put it, but I could not find it anywhere. I searched the entire wardrobe, but I could not find it. My mind was flooded by anger and I started shouting. I entered another room, where the lady that had ironed Antonija's dress was, I asked her if she had seen anything unusual. She said that she saw a couple entering the house. When she went to check, the woman was standing in front of the doors. When the woman who was supposed to be ironing the dress asked the women in front of the doors what was happening, she answered that her man was very drunk and she was minding him. I knew that he liked to steal so that was enough for me, and he was not that drunk anyway. It is interesting that he was about to head home just as we found out. I ran after him to stop him and I attacked him to get my money back. That is where I made a mistake. I should have just checked him in front of a witness. Unfortunately, the anger in me was stronger. We somehow ended up in the house and pandemonium started. He was denying that he took anything, so my neighbour and I confronted him. I went crazy and started punching him. People tried to calm me down and I went into the room where the money was kept. In the room, I punched through a closed window and I cut my right forearm. People were calming me down and were telling me to go to the hospital, because I was bleeding a lot, but all I wanted was my money. Somehow, in all that panic, my wife found the money on the floor beside the broken window. How the money ended up there was always a mystery, but I believe that the man's wife took the money there and threw it on the ground. And that was how my wedding became a bloody wedding. I am honestly sorry today that I went crazy, but I could not help myself. It was not the first time that I got into a fight with someone when I was drunk. It happened a few times innocently, but I was very violent especially when I was drunk. A person teased me a lot and I broke his nose in front of 15 people and nearly ended up in jail. The injustice hurt me back then, but I always resolved it with fights.

Today, I resolve injustice with acceptance and take care of myself. That is the way of karma and the law of cause and effect works, so if I have injustice in my life, I take care of myself with honest words. The effect is then always on the side of the person who is unjust. I will give you an example, because it is in my heart and I resolved the situation. It recently happened, because at the time, I was living in Ireland. What happened was that I got an offer to have tenants live in my house in Croatia. With an open heart, I wanted to go and help them as much as I could. At the time of making the contract, I did not want to make the rent high out of compassion and because one of the tenants said that she would take care of the house. I told her that the house was okay and that she only needed to take care of small jobs. I also told her that trust is difficult to build but easy to take down. She told me that she was like that too and that I had nothing to worry about. I gave her all my trust to mind the house.

Recently, I travelled from Ireland with my family to spend the holidays there, and we ended up spending most of the time working on things that had not been done but we were told had been done. In my eyes, that was a lie and a false presentation. I am a tenant here in Ireland and I would not do anything like that, because it is someone else's property and it should be kept as clean as if it were your own. I gave the person three months to find a new place to live, because I do not agree with disrespect and lies. In my reality, because my intuition was on a higher level, lying was mental abuse for me. You should know that whoever I get in contact with, I tell them that. Only with the truth can we come to our true essence and to the God Creator.

Let us move on to a period after the wedding. I was not raised properly and neither was my Antonija. I was saying that she was mine, in a way that meant that she was my companion and not that she was my property. She never was, and never will be. The old belief patterns are that a woman is beneath the man. I will tell you that a woman is as equally worthy as any man. We are all creatures made by God and there is no difference other than our genders and looks. The rest is the same, but our beliefs and our upbringing are quite different through various judgements. I am not for chauvinism and I am not for feminism. I am for the balance of these energies because we each are two beings, and every man has a female side from their mother in them and a male side from their father in them, and it's the same with women. Our left side of our body is female, and our right side is male. You can check that if you look at the fingers on your hand, or to be more accurate, the pointer fingers and then compare them. You will see that one is more feminine than the other. It is the same with your mind. It has a feminine and masculine energies. With the brain, it is reversed, which means that our right side of our brain is female and is our creative energy, and the left side of our brain is the logical side. You can see that we are constantly spinning around the balance and that it is not good to be on either side of the brain for too long. If we are in the middle, we become one with ourselves and the Creator.

With most men, the feminine side needs to be balanced to be more precise and, for most women, the masculine energy needs to be more balanced. That is why some men are more connected to the feminine energy and are out of balance with their male energy, and vice versa with women. All these things are possible to heal if we see the problem in them. If you do not see the problem in something, your soul has decided that to have that kind of experience is completely fine. The best thing to do is to not be strict towards yourself. Everything you do is completely fine and everything in this life is an experience. If you let the problem in through a bad feeling, then your energy is pushing you to work on yourself. The Universe guides you every day through feelings.

A lot of people do not know how to solve problems on their own, so they turn to alternative healing methods where serious shifts in consciousness and in life can happen. You should know that if you are working on yourself, you are helping to heal this planet and your genetic line. That thought along with other things was what pushed me into the darkest corners of my subconscious so that I could find my healing.

I've wandered off again, but if feel that it was necessary for you.

Thanks to Dražen and Mirko, the farmers where I worked, I started working on my own plumbing after the wedding. Me and Antonija wanted to buy a TV, but they changed our minds. You see how I nearly went the same way as my parents did, but thank God that I was smarter and that I had people in my life who guided me. Dražen said that he would teach me how to do plumbing and that if I was stuck that he would help me. I picked it up quickly. I did the plumbing in the house and installed a bath that my parents had bought – they used fire to heat the water. After that, nothing special really happened other than the feeling that I was cursed. Every month after the wedding, I had situations where I fell into depression because I experienced loss and had arguments that I did not want to happen.

I will give you an example: Antonija went to the hospital to give birth. I was working and I had a lot of work with pigs that we had for sale. My dog ran away and killed most of my neighbour's chickens while he was out drinking. He was abusing me while drunk and he wanted to kill the dog. I did not let him, and I offered to give him my chickens instead. He was violent and wanted to kill the dog no matter what. I ran into the house with the dog and locked myself in there. The neighbour kept knocking on my door and I had to call the police. Later, when he had sobered up, we both got fined in court. I even drove him with me to court. I often asked myself if I was cursed because nothing went the way I wanted it to. I tried living differently and being smarter, but I could not stop those things.

If I could go back in time, I would say that the dark energies that I was in touch with were doing it. Antonija and I watched horror movies every day. I was also addicted to pornography. Remember, when I was younger, I looked at naked pictures. I was hiding it from Antonija when I was doing it, but I never let it affect my relationship with her. We had sex regularly. I will never forget that year, 2003, because at the end of the year, I got my child that I have today. A son that we called Leonardo. We gave him that name because my star sign is a Leo and my son is my heir.

I will never forget that I have given him distress and traumas without realising that I had done it. I was talking about myself and the birth. Unfortunately, I abused Antonija whilst she was pregnant. I know that that harmed him, but I really did not know what I was doing and I could not help myself. When he was born, the birth took eight hours. Yes, you heard me right. In the Bjelovar hospital, they did not care about women or their pains. They could have performed a caesarean section straight away and not torture her the entire time she was in labour. It was not even that bad, until Leo stopped breathing, then they quickly removed him, via caesarean section. Leo was literally dead for five minutes without me knowing. Thank God, they brought him back to life and the nurse brought him to me so that I could see him. He had a weird-shaped head, like a mushroom, because he got stuck in the channel between the pelvis and his head was deformed. Because I did not know much about births, I was shocked.

Today, I know that he did not want to come into this world, and that he did not let himself come out, just like me. It did not help that I had brought a lot of trauma, because I vigorously rejected him at first sight, which was exactly what my mother had done to me too. History was repeating itself and I was unaware of it, but you should know that, back then, I was just an ordinary working-class man who did not believe in anything other than the church. I even thought that the Indian chakras were stupid until I discovered the absolute truth. My son, when you read this book, forgive me, please. I've told you countless times that my actions towards you were not conscious and that I always wanted the best for you. There was more, but I will talk about it later.

Throughout the next two weeks, I started to love this little miracle of nature. I must be honest that that first encounter shocked me so much that it took me a while to begin loving him. I know that it sounds weird, and I do not know if it happens to other men, but I believe that this happened for a reason, because Leonardo's energy was that he did not feel welcomed into this world because of my behaviour. I have written all of this with full honesty so that if you are ever a parent, you should watch your behaviour if you want your child to be good in life and if you want it to accomplish something. People let children do whatever they want with the excuse that they are just children, but you should know that every mistake is exposed when the children are older. That is when parents commonly blame the children, when they are responsible really, or maybe they do not want to recognise their oversight. Did you know that telling a child "No" is classed as abuse if you do not explain the reason behind it? Did you know that it is abuse if the child wants to speak and you do not allow them to speak because you are having a conversation with someone else?

Yes, all of it is psychological abuse on an unconscious level. Remember that I said that children are like a programmable computer, or like an empty container into which you and the environment where the child lives are being poured, together with the emotions and experiences that eventually lead to all kinds of unplanned bad situations, which can even lead to serious psychological and physical diseases. If you already are a parent and if you recognise yourself in this, you should know that there is a medicine for everything and everything can be fixed. First, you must change your behaviour. Second, your children could do some kinds of alternative methods of healing, because the alternative methods of healing are becoming more popular around the world. Why am I just mentioning alternative methods? Because we are spiritual beings in a material world. Everything is energy and we know that energy can be transformed.

I have been in this spiritual world for almost eight years, and I can see significant shifts in my own consciousness. A lot of people today turn to themselves. As I said, everything happens for a reason. The reason for this shift is that we register more from the material world and then move towards the spiritual world. I do not know if you know about the ancient Incas and Mayas? I deeply feel that they ascended, or to be more truthful that they changed their vibrations and disappeared from this world. I would say that this world is in a state of purgatory and that we are here to be cleansed and to learn how to find ourselves or our true nature, which is our connection to God. Before anything, it is a requirement for us to have a lot of wishes, to persistently forgive, to love, to accept, to sympathise and to be good.

That was how we lived as a small family with my grandfather in the same house. I spent most of my day working. The more traits I learnt from the people where I worked, the more I created. That all started happening after the priest came to my house to bless it. I asked him to take the curse from us because nothing worked out for us. The priest, Nikola, was a particularly good and noble man. People say today that all priests are bad, but I would not categorise them because that is the ego mind. This man was good and he served God. He even helped my family after my brother's death by donating money to us.

He blessed us and everything started going well. Now, what happened was that I had concluded that the reason everything was fixed was because of our faith in him and his faith in God. Usually, we all have a spark in us and we believe what Jesus said:

"Your faith has saved you."

You should know that I am not a powerful person and that my only power is just the faith that I have learnt throughout the years, and you too can learn it. You have unlimited power in your heart, and you can do everything, but you need to open that power by believing in yourself.

How?

As a child, you learn to walk or ride a bicycle. Slowly, you practise and are persistent. I highly recommend some work with an alternative healing technique which you resonate with. Just start and do it.

When everything started going properly, we wanted to build something so that we could breed pigs for sale. My grandfather was stubborn, and he did not agree with our ideas. He was the pillar of the family, so a lot of people said that he was the boss. Unfortunately, it was not a tradition to listen to older people and older people grew up differently in Croatia than in Colombia. In Colombia people are living more in their hearts and are connected to their families, but in Croatia it's the opposite. I took the lead on a more difficult way.

One night, after a hard day of working, I came home. I was outside with my grandfather and I told him our plan. He was stubborn and did not let us start working. I blew up and I grabbed him by his shirt under the neck and proved to him that he needed to give in. I did not hit him, but it was a fight, like the animals in the wilderness, a fight for dominance. Maybe I should not have acted like that, but it happened. I had paid my grandfather's bills and his old way of life was unbearable. Antonija and I had a vision that she would raise the pigs at home and that I would work, so that she had some type of work because she did not finish school and she did not have a chance to find any work nearby. After that situation, my grandfather went to the social service and asked for a place in a nursing home. I told him that he should not go and that I would take care of him. That night, I had frightened him and he was scared that I would start beating him. I did not want that and I would not do that. I just wanted him to let us do whatever we wanted. After all, the house and all the buildings were our inheritance and would be ours when he passed.

I will talk a bit about nursing homes in Croatia. There is a high level of corruption and a lot of people come to power through fame and money. My grandfather was in a nursing home where he lived on the top floor. The stairs were very steep, and even I found it hard going up the stairs during visits. We came to see him and the food he was given was half of what he used to eat. The woman who owned the place even shouted at the residents. There was one man who did not like the soup. She said that he must eat it because he was not going to get anything else. When I saw what kind of environment that my grandfather lived in, I did my best to try and persuade him to come back home to us. I promised him a warm home, food and everything that he needed. I just asked him to let us do what we wanted. He accepted my offer and came home. As I am on the topic of nursing homes in

Croatia, I would like to say that old people are still people and that they are the generation who raised our society. Old people deserve more than they get, they deserve our gratitude, care, respect and nice words. Old people are like children and they just want peace. It is up to us to give them that peace and to give them everything that they need to live the last days of their lives with dignity. I believe that people who own nursing homes that are not well run are separated from the heart and they think with their minds. They look at the profit that they get from those people. There is no humanity, no justice. We all deserve equality no matter if we are young or old. We all deserve to be loved and accepted.

Throughout life, I learnt that everything can be solved with nice words in a peaceful way without arguing, but a certain amount of bravery is needed and so is the connection with your heart. If we are talking from our hearts then there are no arguments, but instead, it is a calm way and kind words are used to come to a compromise.

Easy for me to say, yeah?

You need to do it. If you do not try it, you will not accomplish anything. I will give you an example. If you do not agree with your partner's behaviour, say that you barely see them because they are at work, it is not good to start a story with questions like:

"Why are you working so much?" and "Why do you leave me alone?", etc.

In that way, you are turning on your mind's defence system and your mind is in charge, not your heart. That is when the arguments start, and everything is upside down.

How do you act then?

When you come home, take a moment and do not just attack like a bomb, because the person might have had a hard day full of stress at work. You do not want them to take out all their stress on you. Try saying something like,

"Dear, when you are away, it is so hard for me to be alone."

You can add things that you feel in those moments, that is, what you feel, not what you think. Then ask,

"Can you do something so that we can be together more."

Do you see the difference as you read? It might even remind you of at least one situation from your past when this could have prevented an argument. It is also necessary to be honest at the very beginning because you gather heavy energies in you that can harm your health and, of course, your relationship. Later, when it all builds up inside you, you end up taking it all, if not even more, out on the other person. That is why you need to be honest. Talk honestly and base your relationship on the truth. Those are the strongest foundations which you can create in your relationship and that is how love will survive. Love cannot exist if you gather fear, anger, hatred and resentment towards your partner. A lot of people will say that they do not resent or hate. Believe me, if you get angry often, you automatically start resenting. Every denial that you do not have something in you already says that you do have it. Be honest with yourself. If you are not, then you will not get rid of those emotions. Remember, love is an opposite emotion to the other ones. When you become aware of your emotions, then you are one step closer to letting go of them.

How to let go of feelings?

There are a lot of ways to do that with alternative healing techniques or just by closing your eyes and letting yourself feel those emotions by visualising the situation. You can imagine how light is fixing everything that is not necessary from your relationship and your system.

So, that is how we became a family again. My grandfather was with us and everything was as I'd promised. Nothing really happened after that, and everything was going to plan. I can say that even though I was violent towards Antonija, we did have some nice moments together. My grandfather did not live long after he came back home and after a few months, he died alone in a hospital.

Unfortunately, I made a mistake and I made myself suffer. Because I always worked and I wanted more work, I neglected him in the hospital. We found him unconscious after he had had a stroke, and he would not wake up. I was with him twice and, I complained to the nurse why is he connected to the machine that kept him alive. I didn't want him to suffer. Somehow my feeling was that he did not want to be in this world anymore. My biggest regret was when I found out that our loved ones hear us when we are nearby, even if they are unconscious. I regretted that I went to work every day and that I did not go to visit him after work to comfort him, so that he was not alone. During healing, I cried so many tears so that I could heal my heart from all that sadness and regret. You see, today, a lot of people chase a career and money, and they forget the same things I did – our loved ones and our families.

Later, we regret that we did not do something differently. We can do things differently, but we need to sort out ourselves differently. It is best to listen to your feelings and to connect with yourselves. That is when our feelings lead us in life, and we know exactly what is good and what is bad for us. That is why you should live your own life as if it is your last day alive.

I have a feeling that I should tell you how I managed to change my mother without her doing anything other than agree to my truth.

I was 35 years old. During a meditation, I understood that my mother never told me the words "I love you". It was a big and heavy recognition in my life. I teared up and then started crying. That was when I was in the process where I was becoming aware of my love towards myself. In my life, I act immediately with no delays, so I called my mother in tears. It was impossible to go to her and talk to her in person, because at the time, I lived in Ireland and she lived in Croatia. I told her in tears that she never told me that she loved me. She told me three times that I know of that she loved me, but I told her to say the words,

"I love you" and not "you know that I love you".

It is not the same. That is why my mother accepted without being forced to tell me that she loved me. I started crying even more then. The emotions of sadness from before and the happiness from that moment were mixed up. I told her in tears,

"I love you mother and thank you."

Later, I asked her if we could create a rule that we would always say, "I love you" to each other.

At the start, I wanted to see if she would do it, and I would say, "Do you remember what we agreed to do?"

After a few times, she started saying it more on her own, and she started saying that she loved Antonija and Leonardo, her grandson. You see how through honest communication, you can accomplish a result that you wished for. That is what we feel or what we miss in life. Everything can be accomplished, but it is up to us to decide if we want to change ourselves and, in doing so, change others as well. Please do not force these kinds of things, but when you feel that you need to, then be direct and honest. The result will always be on your side.

10.

With Gratitude Towards Law Of Attraction

Let's go on with my life again and what was happening afterwards. This book is about my life and all wisdom that I've gathered. I have so much to share and to write, but I cannot manage it all in one book. I will follow my feelings and what comes from the heart. That was how it became just the three of us in a relatively big house that needed renovating, because we had a lot of damp and dirt where we were planning on having the bathroom. We started to work hard to earn as much money as we could so that we could have a decent house and living. Because I had bonded with the farmers who had beautiful houses, I wanted to have something like that too. The only way then was to work hard. I worked on cutting trees to sell and I worked in the fields. I worked for six days a week, ten hours per day. There were no options other than agriculture and working late at night. We worked on the trees on Sundays and during the winters when there was less work. We managed to earn a fair bit of money, but it was extremely hard for us. Thank goodness we were young, so we managed to endure it. I could say that we cut down record-breaking metres of trees a day.

One winter while working, we came up with the idea that we should start a nursing home. Honestly, we had money on our minds. That is how we slowly started to do up the interior of the house for a nursing home. We worked normally as usual and we now worked with old people too. It was Antonija's job to care for them while I had to work at my job.

That was when hard times occurred for pig farmers and we slowly started getting rid of our pigs. We kept a few for personal needs. Unlike the other nursing homes, we took care of those people with the dignity they deserved. We had a clean house, peace, food, and the freedom of movement and family visits. All because of our wish or, in other words, our greed, we considered making even more money, so we moved into a room that was 16 square metres, where the three of us lived and slept. It had all our furniture in it. We could have had four people in our house. The original plan was that we would do up the top floor of the house and live there, and that the elderly would be on the bottom floor of the house. We lived like rats in that room for around a year. Winter came and I made a decision and said,

"We can't live like this anymore. I don't know how, but we are moving upstairs next year."

We did not have much money, but we had enough. I had a plan that we could make money by selling wood, but it was not enough.

Now, I will show you how the Creator works. February came and an old grandmother who nearly froze in her house came to us. Antonija gave the highest care to her and the others. The grandmother had savings, a house and land in her name. After some time, the God in her started talking. She said:

"My dear, I will give you everything when I die."

She said that constantly for over two weeks. Because this was an opportunity for all of us and her distant family did not want anything, we went to an insurance company to ask the attorney. As it was the grandmother's free will and because she was of sound mind and was healthy, they agreed to make a contract. In the past, we were a social case, so the principal was of great help. Thank you for that and thank you to the notary public. So, the grandmother signed everything over to Antonija and not long after the contract was signed, she died. We did everything that we agreed to, and we gave her a decent burial and we granted all her wishes before and after she died.

Suddenly, we came into some assets, so that we had the money to build the top part of the house. We started it immediately. That next year, we made the decision to move up into the new part of the house. My understanding through life is not just shown here, but there were many other situations where I decided that enough was enough and that I needed something different, and everything was put into place the way it should have been. What was necessary was that I needed to know what I wanted, that is, what I wanted if I was not happy with my life. Wealth exists everywhere and we all deserve things equally. You are just limiting yourself with poor programmes. I have a need to say that I regretted tearing down forests, but I worked hard to build my house. Within a few years, I ended up in Ireland with my family, also because of money. I was not planning on going back, because all the money and effort was failing in Croatia. For every evil, there is some good or a good lesson. My lesson was that I wished my life so much to be like that of others that I lost myself. In the same way, I built an objective where instead of enjoying life together with my family, we did not even "live" anymore. We had to take care of older people, so we could not afford even two or three days of vacation.

Just work, work, work. That is why I am saying that you should put yourself and your needs first, through listening to your feelings, and then the houses, apartments and other material things will come in an order. Enjoy life because you only have one life in this reality, so use it well. Be as good as you can towards yourself and your closest ones, and you will feel more fulfilled than if you chased after a career. We all have something creative in us and, in that way, you can derive pleasure when you do that. Today, a lot of people do what they do not like and that separates them from their heart, and it makes them incredibly stressed. That was happening to me too.

Today, I have found out what I love to do, and I am fulfilled and happy when I do it, but this is a different topic and I will possibly keep most of it for another book, because I was in a completely different state of existence before that. I am going to keep it a secret that you will maybe read in the second book.

I told you that I did not enjoy life with my family, but in Croatia, it is tradition that the woman is at home and that the man goes out a lot. It is not a rule, but it happens a lot. I used to find some free time and I would go out with my friends to a tavern and, of course, I almost never came home sober. I know that it was not right towards Antonija and it was not right towards a lot of other women. I would say that it was one of the biggest reasons for arguments in a family.

I need to go back a bit now. I will be as honest as always. Dražen had a beautiful wife, Vesna. I found her incredibly attractive, even though Antonija was a beauty. Something in me was attracted to Vesna. So that we are clear, I did not do anything with Vesna, but the fire in me burned for her. I believe that her partner noticed that, but because there was nothing physical, he did not care.

What happened?

Today, I know exactly why it was that I wanted Antonija to dye her hair blonde and to have similar hair as Vesna. I asked Antonija to dress like her too. Somehow, Vesna was an example of what a woman should look like. You see what kind of trap I fell into. After healing, I understood why I was like that. Because I did not have a proper family. I worked for a good and wealthy family, and I started picking up their patterns of behaviour. The illusion was that I would succeed like they did if everything in my life was the same or similar as theirs.

I know that that was crazy in some way, but my entire past was crazy and my mind was not the clearest. Today, I see that it is wrong to follow others. We are all individual beings and Creators. That is when it helped me to succeed in life as I always believed I could, but those were just material things. I was addicted to material things and money. A lot of people say that that belief is not right. Money does not corrupt people; money gives power to those people and they misinterpret the energy of money, and then they act the way that they truly are. They are not wearing "masks" anymore because they "have" power. I will tell you simply that money is not power.

The real power is having harmony with yourself and with God. That is the true power that we all need to have. When we have that, money comes from familiar and unfamiliar sources.

We just need to listen to our hearts and our inner direction and unconditionally accept it and give. That is how I slowly wandered into the world of material things and, of course, learnt a lesson from everything. I did not know that the world worked like that before, but I still learnt by my own and other people's mistakes. I believe that I had that naturally in me and later it was shown to me that I had. The biggest thing that ever happened to me was again created from the law of attraction, even though I did not know about that. Thanks to all the hard work, I finally had enough money to buy a car. I will tell you the story from the beginning. I had peers who worked in a company together and all three of them bought used cars that were seven years old at the time. At the time, I had an old but good car. In my village, the energy is that everyone must be better than each other and I also worked in that kind of place. You should know that those people do not know any better. I believe that people are constantly competing consciously and subconsciously with whoever is going to have the better car, more land and better machines. I did not feel jealous of my friends or their cars. I felt regret because I did not have anything like that. Me and Antonija smoked cigarettes. One day, I calculated how much money we could save so we could buy a new car if we stopped smoking. We decided to stop smoking with no help other than our willpower and a wish for a better, healthier life.

Dražen and Mirko decided to raise my wages so that, at the bank, it would look good and I could ask for a loan. I did everything with them honestly according to an agreement. I looked at a lot of middle-class cars, but the one that I was attracted to the most was the Seat Leon. I read some newspapers where there was an old Leon and I really wished for it. It was called a lion in the same way as my star sign. I did not tell anyone other than the people I worked with until it was 100% happening. I wanted to show that I was worth something. I know that everyone was telling me that I would fail and that nothing good would become of me. I felt as if I was working despite everyone and that I wanted to subconsciously prove them wrong. I managed to order the car and I was so excited that I ended up going to the garage most days just to look at the model there. The salesperson even wanted me to buy a cheaper and less powerful car, called an Ibiza, but I wanted the Leon. It was a 2007 car and I suspect that you all know what it looks like. It is still beautiful today. It looked like a real lion and it is honestly a miracle the way that the people made it.

Now, I will show you an example of lust, which was quite common in our little community. Later, I told this one boy that I'd bought a Leon, and he said that that car was worthless. I asked him why. He said because the wipers wipe inwards, not like the wipers on the usual cars, which wipe outwards. A lot of people did not even believe it at first that I had bought a car like that. Remember that, in their minds, I was a nothing and a nobody. The day came and we went to collect the car. I was so happy that I bought licence plates with my date of birth on them. It was black, fast and it was a great car, one of the best cars in the place where I lived. I had not felt that happy at all before that day and I kept feeling happy with the car for a long time.

Later, when I had found out about the law of attraction and how the Universe works, I remembered that I had looked at the car from the side. My godfather once had a Suzuki Swift when I was 13 and it was the first sports car in the village. I loved that car and often imagined myself having it. I visualised it and felt that it was mine. The rims, the colour and the shape. From that moment, I came to realise that the Leon looks a lot like the car I visualised in my childhood. I believe that it was the Creator trying to show me that I am the Creator of my own life. That I can create everything, but also to take Him into my life unconditionally. Today, I am very thankful to the Creator for giving me that car, even though some challenges started to appear with the car, which I will talk about. I will divert your attention now to one of the biggest virtues that a person can have and that is gratitude.

I intentionally did not write about it sooner. Did you ever ask yourself whether everything in this life is a blessing? Are you grateful for your life?

I am incredibly grateful for everything that has happened in my life, good and bad. The good made me happy and the bad taught me to become better, and it pushed me to change so that I could become what I am today. You should know that today I am not perfect, but I've turned my life around and I've made massive changes to my subconscious and my behaviour. I am not perfect, as I also sometimes wander off because different stories attract me.

Now, as I am writing this book, I have concluded that if I want to keep in this state of my consciousness, I need to be careful when selecting my company and the topics that people talk about. I am currently learning, and I know that I will get that chance sooner or later. I am usually a very empathetic person and I can put myself in everyone's shoes. I understand people but I also know that I do not have the right to change anyone.

That is where the obstacles in me are created. I see how people treat each other today, with lust, anger, resentment, gossip and, worst of all, is the way that people treat Mother Earth. A lot of people take this planet for granted. They are putting the blame on someone else. In cities, trash is flying around, nature is full of rubbish everywhere. You see it is not all my responsibility, but I try my best to collect other people's trash when I see it in nature. I have concluded that parents do not teach their children that trash does not belong in nature. That kind of behaviour makes me sad, and it weighs heavily on my heart. Being in the presence of people who are in the low vibration also collapses my vibration. I have nothing against those people. They will find someone like them, and I will just be with my family if I must.

I will go back to gratitude.

Have you ever been honestly grateful for the glass of water that you drink or the food that you eat?

These things should keep us happy and joyful.

Why?

This world is out of balance and I will give you the example of two countries. America chases after money and fame, and a lot more money. In restaurants, they serve 2 litres of Coca-Cola with a big meal, while they are still getting obese, and they throw food away while there are people in Africa who are dying from starvation.

I hope that you understand that I am writing this without judging, but I am showing you the imbalance in our society. Everything happens for a reason and so do those situations. A good example for me is to spend the minimum, and I always explain to my child with an example why he needs to eat everything that he puts on his plate. Food is sacred and we need to respect it and be grateful for it. I gave him an example of children in Africa and the deaths that happen every day because of hunger. That is why the things that are around us can be particularly good teachers and they can show us that we can be grateful for everything that we have.

I know that you are asking yourself why it is that God does nothing about it, when injustice is happening. Many forget about karma and the law of cause and effect. I deeply believe that those who lived a life without respect and took from others come back to those bodies so that they can learn their lesson, or to be more precise, so their soul can learn a lesson. Souls evolve and learn in this world. Through learning, the soul has free will, which later can be overturned by the mind, resulting in envy, jealous, intemperance, plunder, murder, rape, violence and crimes. Again, this soul has the support of the Creator and free will, but it takes the consequences of the law of cause and effect.

You should know that it is not my intention to scare you or to try to change you. My intention is to explain to you that if you want harmony with the Creator, your behaviour must be more positive and you can try to change, not just for yourself, but for the world in general. As I said before, this thought was brought to me through feelings and a vision. I told you that I am not usually very visual, but sometimes in moments of healing, I get visions mixed with emotions. I also do not know why a vision comes to me much clearer when my eyes are open as an awareness, than when my eyes are closed. It is hard to explain, but I know that some of you know what I am talking about. I wanted to say that I remembered my healing from my past lives. As I studied, I resonated with the truth. All our past lives are just a copy of our current one. In my past lives, I was unfortunately a culprit and a rapist, a warrior, a priest and a shaman. That is all that I am getting now, probably because it is important.

I will tell you how I healed the offending past. It was extremely hard. I saw myself with a black cape and there were two more people beside me. It was a kind of cult where I cut off some man's head. That was extremely hard for me to find out, that I did that kind of evil to someone. I took away a life. I hated myself, and I cried in those moments of healing. After I managed to heal myself, I asked the Creator for unconditional love and healing. That was all possible because I wanted to heal it and face myself and my feelings. Thank goodness that through Theta Healing, it all went fast, and the traumas and other feelings do not last long. It is cleansing in a fast and effective way.

That is how you can see that a lot of the things were reflected in my past and that I lived a similar life. I did not kill anyone, but unfortunately though, I did hurt people and make some bleed. I can tell you that violence is the same as murder. Every bit of violence kills a part of God in that person and the person loses their sense of identity. They lose themselves; they supress themselves. As I am on the topic of violence, I will talk to you about the worse thing I have done in my family. There is a lot of it. Because I inherited the patterns of behaviour from my parents, I was very quarrelsome in the family and I was extremely strict with my son, Leonardo. Over every mistake that he made, I would physically punish him. At the start, it was just an easy tap on the hands, but later, I started to beat him and slap him, and such. I am so sorry for doing that. At the time, I believed that it was for his own good. I was not very conscious of the consequences that it will have in his future. I was incredibly young, and I still did not feel good within myself but I was not aware of what my parents had done to me. I will tell you the first big punishment I gave him.

We were in a store and we were standing at the till. He really wanted something from the shelf, and he started crying and screaming for it. We ignored it, but I was boiling inside. All the spoilt children went through my head and I did not want to have a spoilt son. We did not buy him anything and we got in the car. He was around five years old then. When we got in, he was in the back seat and I was in the driver seat. I turned around and slapped him so hard that he fell on the seat. I was so full of anger in the same way that my father was. I told Leonardo that that was the last time he would embarrass me in public. I know that this is hard for you to read, but you should know that this is hard for me to write as well.

You understand this now?

Since that situation, Leonardo has not asked for anything to be bought for him. He has lived through and with that trauma for years and he is very humble. I did not want to do it, nor was it my intention, but I did it. I forgave myself for what I did, but I would do anything for him to forgive himself and me, and for him to become different. As you can see, violence is murder. I killed a part of him with that violence. Today, I see that it is an important part of him because he is dependent on us and when we tell him to buy something for himself he does. He does not ask us for money unless we offer it to him. I told him a lot of the time that he can see that I am different now and he should let go of the fear, but he is still in fear a lot. I believe that, in the future, he will find the strength and go on the path of healing the things that I have mostly caused him. I hope he will understand that this was an experience. His deeply rooted fear, the fear that he will be punished has been rooted into his subconscious and only he can fix it. I believe in free will, and I cannot force him to heal himself. He has decided to live like that.

You should know that when I started to heal myself, I told him a lot of times that I loved him and that I was sorry. If he ever wants to heal himself, I will pay for everything for that healing. I regretted doing those things to him. Once when he had bad grades in school, he lied about it because he was scared. I took him out of the house when he was eight years old in his t-shirt into the freezing weather. I did not want him to lie, and I was not aware that I had caused him suffering before. I knew that it was hard for him and now I am writing this in tears because I can feel what he felt and I can see him now so little freezing out in the cold. I cannot believe that I did something like that to such a beautiful little being, full of kindness, and that I caused him to feel fear. Leonardo, forgive me please. I did not know better. I am sorry and I love you. I love you as if I am you and you are me. I hope that you find the strength to heal the distress and traumas that I have given you. I will be at your side whenever you need me.

The third time when I caused him damage was when I was already aware about everything, but the new work and new environment completely took me away from my heart. He was already older now, around 12 years old. We were in Ireland. It was incredibly stressful because all I did was work and come home. Because of all that stress, I started to drink alcohol. I was not drunk then, but after an eight-hour shift and stress at work, I was faint-hearted. He broke the printer and the ink that I bought for it. We wanted to earn money and we were thinking about every single penny. In my head, it was a massive loss of money. I went crazy and I started shouting, as if I were obsessed. I shouted so much until my anger exploded. That was when I grabbed him by the neck and pushed him onto the bed. I will never forget what he did in response, and I am so sorry from the bottom of my heart. When I held him by the neck and when I was strangling him, he completely let go, he went limp, as if he would let me kill him.

Now, you see as I am writing this exactly how the things that I did not forgive myself for happened. Believe me, it is hard now and my tears of regret are pouring down my face as I remember those moments. The thing that is coming to me is that I've healed myself and now I have a lot of compassion, and when I remember those things, I can feel what it was like to be him in those moments. I can feel that he had had enough of my abuse, that he had had enough of life, and that he hated himself and his actions. He hated that he was stupid and kept disappointing me. You should know that that situation was a mutual creation, because he often said that he felt like a disappointment to us, so he created those kinds of thoughts. I made him like that with my belief that he was sloppy Leonardo, that he was always breaking something. You see how our beliefs are limited in life and how we create reality?

It is all about perception and, today, I have a lot more energy for accepting others and him. It is all a thing of acceptance and compassion. There is a law of compassion, which is my primary law today. It is a law that my soul must master.

What does that mean?

Find balance in compassion. In other words, I was either too hard on my son as you read earlier on, or I am too compassionate, so I start feeling too much, every detail, which is what you also read earlier. The last time that I attacked him, it was so violent that when I was going to work, I cried so much and regretted what I did. The next day, I asked him to forgive me and told him that I loved him. He never rejected my forgiveness, stubbornly or through his pride. He always accepted my apology. I have to say that I am so grateful to the Creator for the fact that I have him in my life. Everybody who knows him says that he is such a good child, which is true. There were a lot of similar situations like those, but those were the worst ones. I would not burden myself with that, because it was always the same thing. He was scared and so he lied. I wanted him not to lie and to be good and obedient. He was obedient and diligent. I was the one who wanted to have a perfect son. That is where I made a mistake, because there is no such thing as perfect and we all make mistakes. They are needed for us to learn from them.

I was lacking a lot of patience and acceptance that he was so young and that he could not immediately be like me, which was my wish. To me, it was enough to make a mistake once and it would not happen again. Because I was coming from my perspective and my mind expected others to be like that too. What my mind did not know back then was the differences and the degree of consciousness of a certain person. Today, after many years of working on myself, I have learnt that I have gathered a lot of wisdom. Wisdom is not to know the things that you have read, wisdom is what you feel in your heart and your personal visions, or when you come to a moment when it clicks in your mind and you go "AHA", and you have that epiphany. We all have wisdom in our hearts. Our minds are the only obstacle to accessing our wisdom. We are here to collect experiences, to learn from one another, to teach each other and to remember who we are, that is, that we are one with God. That would mean that we are here to find God. For a soul, that is the highest degree and that is when the soul can decide if it wants to go back to this degree of existence. The soul can choose if it will come back as a spiritual teacher like Jesus or to stay in the higher spheres and serve the Creator.

I am going to return to my car, which has brought me so much happiness but also brought a lot of challenges to my relationship with Antonija. I was young and good looking, and I had a sports car. I was around 27 years old. The best years, but I was married. I had a lot of girls in my life, but something in me wanted more. I used to go out with my friends and there were a lot of situations where girls liked me. I gave into temptation and I started cheating on Antonija with other girls. Antonija did not even know that, because I disguised it. I am not proud of that period, but I will later explain what the reason for my behaviour was. I cheated on her around seven times in the span of five years. It was not anything serious, up until the last one, which I will talk about later. That is how I slowly started to live a guy's life and went out more often. I worked, but a lot less because now we had more income, mostly from Antonija. I know that it was not right, but I could not help myself, because in male company and then in company in general and in movies, men cheated on their wives. That was how I became a "cool" guy, and I had some time for a girl every now and again. Of course, everything was followed by alcohol and heavy energies. What I said was that I was hiding but at the same time saying the truth. Listen how crazy I was. If I slept with someone that night, I would come home and Antonija would ask me where I was, and I would say that I was with another girl. She'd laughed and so would I. I know that it was not funny, but it was like that back then. I had a strong sexual energy and I did not neglect Antonija. That was why she was never suspicious of me. I cannot describe with words how grateful I am that she was always full of love towards me, and you see how I returned that love back to her. It was all wrong and no wonder that the Creator tried to show me to stop, because I crashed my car a few times. I did not see it at the time, but I see it now. A car and traffic are life and how to behave, from my point of view. If there is a traffic jam and if I keep coming to a red light, it's usually because I'm going to a place where I would not have a fruitful visit. It is by paying attention to the signs that I have gathered throughout the years. It is the same for me, a car represents me, my status and my life.

The Creator took away that vehicle and tried to stop me a few times with smaller accidents, but I stubbornly continued to be a "cool" guy. I missed that in my younger years because I never had something like that. Antonija is a woman who has a lot of patience and, with a little bit of complaining, she would let me go out. Sometimes she went with me, but I often went on my own. What I learnt along the way is that no matter what girl I was with, none of them was better than Antonija. I did not know why, and I always tried to find the answer. The answer came a few years later when I realised how much I loved her and that a sexual bond mixed with love is the best thing that can happen to a person.

I was out of balance, and under the influence of friends, television and my environment. You see, today, there are a lot of people who use their sexuality and often change their partners, which comes to an imbalance and unnecessary mixing of energies. People are not aware of it and neither was I at the time. They are not aware that when they are in an imbalance, they change partners so that they get confirmation that they are good enough. That is how I started to look for confirmation that I was good enough, from other women. Everything was connected to my relationship with my mother. At the start of our relationship, Antonija thought that she would cheat on me. I was very jealous, and I followed her every step and watched her. I often complained about anything that I noticed. I had a nose for it, or an intuition for energies. Within a short period of time, I reprogramed her, and she stopped looking at other men. How did I know that?

I did not tell you that the first time I met her, I knew by her look that she liked me, but she was in a relationship with my friend Davor and she was his first girlfriend. Believe me, she was incredibly young and inexperienced, and she had impulses like mine. We are all the same. It does not matter if you are a male or female, we are all one. The only things that are different are gender and personalities. Today's society is still divided, and the woman is the one who suffers. The woman is the one who often does not have the right of speech, because the man is the boss. It was the same with me.

Today, I conclude that man and woman represent the society of unity. So, two people beside each other make the pillars of a relationship or the top of the pyramid, and everything else is underneath. There is no instance where one is better than the other. We are equal. If you base your relationship on honesty, kindness, compassion, understanding, love and equality from the start, your relationship will last a lifetime. Believe me, I did not find happiness with other girls. Everything took me back to Antonija. It was my experience, and I do not judge others and their experiences.

Now, I want to go to a period of my life when I was fed up with the corruption in Croatia, because I am an honest man and injustice always hurts me. I tried to have something that was mine, including my own company. Every time I tried, I came up against a wall of politics. It is unfortunate that a country works like that, but if you are not on the political side of the leading party, then you are lightly condemned to live a humble life. There is no respect, just self-interest. I'd had enough of it, and I found out about an organisation called Anonymous. I liked that idea and the idea of freedom and equality. That was when I thoroughly studied what people call conspiracy theories. There were a lot of them, but I only accepted the things that my heart resonated with. I always had a feeling for the truth. At the time, I saw the organisation as a chance for something to change in my country. I believed that the people can be stronger than any political party and that the nation can wake up like I did. That is when I started to go around the nearby town in my new car with an Anonymous mask with the wish that people would wake up and rise against the injustice. I even started to be more active with hacking, so that I could stop government websites. I wanted a better world for everyone and for me.

At the time, it was very current and, in some towns, there were more protesters, but in Bjelovar, there was always a small amount of us. I was desperate and I asked myself why the people complained against authority but would not join us. I did not think that people were scared or that just complaining helped them. Of course, there was no help in that. It was a time that was preparing me for the future. I learnt a lot back then. I saw over the years how many lies were uncovered in the light and who ruled the world. I will leave this topic to you and I will let you research it on your own.

Why was I saying all of this?

Because through that organisation, I found another peer who turned my life upside-down. Her name was Ivana and she was from Zadar. We started to text after I saw that she was very up-to-date and active in groups on Facebook. I asked her if I could copy her picture of an Anonymous mask. That is how we started to text. From the beginning, I saw a like-minded person who was remarkably like me. There was not a day that we did not text each other on messenger. Through time, we fell in a type of love, because I loved what she was doing, while Antonija did not have that kind of life. Antonija is very peaceful, and Ivana was just like me, a little bit wild and attractive. I do not even remember how we came to the topic of meeting in person, but Ivana decided to travel 350km to meet me. I honestly thought that we had something, but she had a husband, and I did not want to get in between them. When we met in Bjelovar in a weekend cottage, we talked a lot about everything and how good it was. There was chemistry and we slept together. Yes, that was the last person who I cheated on Antonija with. Ivana was a blessing and a curse.

How? Read on.

11.

Jealousy

Did you ever ask yourself what is jealousy? Jealousy is the fear of loneliness deep inside of you. There is also a great possibility of projection into another person. My example shows this. Jealousy is the separation of relationships and it has nothing to do with love. It is not true that you need to be jealous in a relationship to show that you love someone. You should know that love is never owned. Love just exists. If you are jealous, you are in fact scared. As time passes, you create what you do not want in life. You will come to situations where you will feel even more jealous, and you will ask yourself why this is happening to you. It happens because the Creator gives us what we transmit into the energetic field.

Now, how to get rid of jealousy?

You can try by accepting and trusting in your partner, and just loving them no matter what. A different way is for you to find an alternative method of healing and, consciously with an intention, you can get rid of that challenge. The decision is up to you. I know that I was very jealous and a heavy manipulator, who was intuitive. Often things happened to me, like I said about men coming into Antonija's life. That is an example of how I created situations so that I would be even more jealous. Unfortunately, because I was a skilled manipulator, which was not right, I knew exactly what I needed to do to manipulate Antonija and keep her for myself, when on the other hand, I did what I did not like her doing to me. I knew that it was not right, but what can you expect from a manipulator?

I know that with the help of intuition, I even managed to reprogram Antonija because I caught her looking at other men the same way she was looking at me when she was with my friend. Today, I know that she has relented and that she has recognised that it was not the right thing to do and that I would notice very easily. In a way, it was positive that I saw those signs, even if it was an important way in which I could resolve things. I used to do it with anger. I resolved things through arguments and control. Today, I know that I could have resolved all those problems just by having a calm conversation, so that I could have found out what other men had that caused her to look at them and not at me. I know that today I live a life without jealousy, and I do not notice that Antonija looks at others. In the same way, I do not notice if anybody is trying to flirt with her.

Why?

Because people around us are just actors and they act the way we believe they are meant to be acting. Everything can be resolved and so can the idea of the world within you and around you.

Sex was not incredibly special with her, but I felt enchanted with her. Ivana had the power of telepathy, and when she showed me proof, I was amazed. She often told me that we were the same. That suited me and I wanted to become like that. She showed me a lot of things that could help me become like that and she told me that she went on some courses so that she could learn better. She told me that she would help me. I was so crazy that I did not even hide it from Antonija that I was cheating on her. She just accepted me like that. She is such a strong woman and her love is amazing. A few days later, I took my family to Zadar to visit Ivana. There was a lot of turmoil. Antonija fell apart because I spent our anniversary with another woman. I wanted Ivana and everything that she was. I honestly fell in love with her and forgot the real love I had towards Antonija. I was bewitched. Zadar was beautiful and Ivana recommended to me that I close my eyes and see what image she was sending into my mind. We had made love in the shallow sea before that. The image came to me. She fell in love with me and I fell in love with her. I thought that she was the woman I wanted to spend the rest of my life with.

A part of me wanted to leave Antonija and the other part of me wanted to be with Ivana. After a telepathic exercise, something weird started to happen inside of me. I have often changed in behaviour. One moment, I would be crying and, in the next moment, I would be smiling and then I would be angry. It was as if my system was collapsing. I did not know what was happening to me and I did not share it with Ivana. After returning from Zadar, her husband realised that we were together, and she even told him. We were even thinking of going to Germany with her children. I know that I was crazy that I wanted to leave my family for a woman with three children. We saw each other once more after Zadar and we made love all night. That was when I had a weird dream. I dreamt that I was her. With those words, "You are me", I woke up. She said,

"Yes dear, we are one."

12.

Spiritual Awakening

What happened to me over a short period of time is hard to believe for a regular person. You should know that I did not know what was happening to me. Overnight, I stopped shouting and I became a very calm and an exceptionally acceptable person. Everybody was surprised at what happened. I started doing research on the internet. I knew that I was not crazy. I knew that if I went to a psychiatrist that he would send me to an asylum. I began to read minds, which my son and Antonija confirmed. In the stores, I heard all the thoughts of people. A huge weariness came over me, as if I were at a concert with no music, just people talking. That is when I started to avoid big halls with people. I looked for an answer for what had happened. I did not know my own identity. I was a Christian who had a strong wish for meditation and inner peace.

I thought that I had to become a Buddhist. A lot of things went through my head. After a while, I realised what had happened to me. I'd gone through a spiritual awakening. On the one hand, I knew that I was special then, and I often looked for peace in nature, that is in the forest. I planned a future with Ivana, but that changed.

How come?

During a meditation, I realised all the things that Antonija does to help me. I also saw that Ivana was totally different than me and that I would eventually have to be her servant. I did not like that scenario, so I ended up staying with

Antonija. I told her this and she was happy and accepted me back. Because I was very calm and I spoke differently than before, Antonija thought that I did not love her anymore. Unfortunately, she suffered in silence.

What happened in the meantime?

Before I left Ivana, Antonija had started texting another man she met at a party. Because my purpose was strong, I realised everything. I found out and I talked her out of it. I was on two sides, I know. Around a month after I stopped my relationship with Ivana, Antonija got together with another man. The Creator did not let me see it at first and He let things happen. Obviously, Antonija was in a big energy to have her revenge. Once I had meditated, the meditation showed me that Antonija had had sex with someone else. I did not see a face, but the feeling was as if it had happened.

It was exceedingly early. I kept waking up every morning at 5, and I meditated and studied spirituality before going to work. When I saw the scene, I opened my eyes and went to talk to Antonija. She denied everything and did not want to tell the truth. I was sure in what I had seen. It is unbelievable how I went to look around the house and I immediately found an old phone that she used to plan meetings. I went to her and asked her to tell me who it was or I would call to find out. She told me who it was, and I felt like I had been stabbed in the back. I will not say much about the person because he was a married man. Now, I felt with every fibre in my body what it was like when someone cheats on you behind your back, which is what I did to her.

What hit me most were two things.

The fact that I was not angry and that it was not just some random man, it was a married man. It was not easy, but I found the power to accept it all and to forgive her. I called that man and told him that if he came close to Antonija again, I would tell his wife but that I forgave him. I was in tears together with Antonija. I told her that I loved her, and she told me that she thought that I did not love her anymore. From that day on, we promised each other something. That we will tell the truth to each other no matter what and that we will share every detail about ourselves so that the only thing that is between us is the truth. We told each other every detail about ourselves. Every truth that we had hidden from each other came to the surface. There was a lot of it, but nothing too scary.

The only thing that was important to me was the truth, because I felt that, in that way, we would create a good foundation for our future relationship. It was a new beginning for us. What I can say is that a life of truth is the only way we can live life honestly and fairly. If you live honestly then you will not have to fear anything and you will not get into uncomfortable situations, because the truth is always revealed. You must know that from your life and from some situations you have been in.

I would like to get onto the topic of pornography again, because I am already on the topic about my companion. Since my mind was very dirty with scenes from pornographic films, of course it was subconscious and we watched a lot of things together, we did not know that, in that way, we were corrupting our heart and souls. Everything was good until I started to drink alcohol. When I drank, perverted thoughts would go through my head. Antonija was always submissive, and I was a skilled manipulator. That was where we were different, and we needed to make a balance. Nobody has the right to manipulate someone else, or to persuade someone to listen to them instead of their hearts and their common sense. I kept trying to persuade Antonija to do all kinds of perversions. I do not want to get into details as I respect her privacy, but if it were about me, I would tell everything with full honesty. To me, it looked as if I was taking advantage of that. Antonija was afraid of me leaving her, so she did everything that I demanded. Thank God, that it all stayed in my imagination and that we never did do anything outside of our relationship. Otherwise, the same thing that happened with me and Ivana could have happened to me and Antonija.

How did I come to everything?

I deeply believe that mixing energies with Ivana is the reason why things started to appear to me and that I started to become like her. I deeply believe that, as souls, we decided to have that kind of experience and that she chose to help me find my true self. In our light, we see good and bad. We adopt our partner, but they are not our property. Everybody has the right to live their life the way they want to live it. Believe it or not, today, I am not jealous, but before I used to be so jealous that I was crazy. Behind jealousy is fear of being alone and distrust in the other person. If you do not have trust in yourself, you cannot have trust in someone else.

Fear originates in the mind and it makes you powerless, and then suddenly situations that you do not want to happen are happening.

Why?

Because your mind places your thoughts connected to fear both consciously and subconsciously. You are the creators here and you create what you think about. Your life witnesses how you live. If there are common arguments in the family then something is not alright with your subconscious mind. It is important that you observe all the details. Observe how you work, what words you say, listen to yourself. Do you know that in a relationship, there is often a reflection or mirroring? Everything that you have is being reflected by your mind in your partner. Often people get into arguments without knowing about reflection. I was like that with Antonija. I will give you an example. I liked a girl. I wanted to be with her, but something inside of me wanted me to stay loyal to Antonija. It was either my common sense or my feelings. My mind fabricated jealousy, that she had someone else too and I attacked her verbally. She defended herself, but I did not believe her.

Why not?

Because my mind wanted to be right, and I wanted another woman and I tried to get what I wanted by arguing. That was just a lie and a trap set by my mind. Antonija went through a lot of bad situations with me, but her honest love and the power of that woman always followed me. It follows me to this day, and I can say that if I ever got a Jackpot, it was the day that I met her, with her honest love and femininity. We are concluding that it is important to be structured and to hold on together. I had the opportunity of witnessing some couples who had good marriages, but they needed to find a compromise and change some things. Of course, stubborn minds do not want to change.

What happened?

Their mind believes that it deserves better and that they will find better, but it forgets that there are lessons in that relationship and that it needs to learn and complete the lessons. What happened was that those marriages fell apart the same way that mine nearly did. Those people got worse partners in their lives after that. They had an even harder life because their energy pushed them to learn in a much more difficult way. At the time, I meditated a lot, so I was warned just in time so that I knew what to do. It was shown to me what would happen, and the decision was up to me. Here you can see the advantage of a spiritual life over a normal life. Of course, everything is life, and nobody is better than someone else. There are just advantages if we go towards ourselves and within ourselves, because that is when we find the traps of the mind and everything that we think that we live.

For us to be able to observe ourselves, we must take complete responsibility for our lives. That means to stop pointing fingers at others around you in any situation. It is necessary to ask yourself what part of you made this person act that way towards you. Perhaps you have had a bad opinion of the person, and you judged them for something (consciously and subconsciously). If someone attacks you, you may think the same way as I used to, that you are nothing and a nobody. There are different situations that you can get into and it is up to you if you want to find the answer. The answer sometimes does not come straight away, but it is eventually shown at the best possible moment. It is necessary for you to be patient and believe in creation. You will never get the answer outside of you, but from within you. In the same way, you can practise trust in yourself and in the Creator in you.

The most important thing that I have learnt in my life is that I am sorry from the bottom of my heart for every argument, threat and physical violence in my family and with other people. I did not mention this, but a lot of people told me that I was like my father and that my father did not give in to himself. He often argued and got in fights with other people. Of course, he was often drunk, and he watched a lot of football games and he cheered for Dinamo Zagreb. That energy led me too. It is the same as everything, it was to learn something and to witness what I learnt. Yes, I learnt that people have the right to choose what they want, but being drunk and arguing, and beating someone because they are not on my side is stupid. Unfortunately, there was a lot of that. Of course, not all people were the same and there are passive fans, but I was on the opposite side. When I think about it, watching others to see who wins is giving them the power to show myself as someone who belongs and is accepted by others. That is why I am asking from the bottom of my heart that you do not make the same mistakes that I did.

Why?

You have a good and honest example of how a person can be lost in the world of drugs, alcohol, pornography, religion and, in the end, how the person finally found himself. At least, I think that I have found myself and the best thing is that you can experience it all and enjoy every day of your life. Every day is a blessing and if we make it sacred in the morning, we have the power to summon the Creator to help us do our best in life. That is when your life will be calm and stable. At least, it was like that for me. But I worked a lot on myself so that I could change myself and become the best version of myself that I can be. I did not run from myself, I faced myself. The best thing that happened later, which I will write in another book, was finding myself.

Let me stay on this.

What I deeply feel is that I will finish with this story now and that I will go deeper into me, which I do daily, and face the world around me – the beautiful planet, full of colours, water, forests and natural riches. If you care in the slightest then make the change so that you waste a minimum amount of water, paper, trees and furniture, because in that way, you are helping the planet and your children and grandchildren. Be aware of your behaviour every day. Do not let your everyday life kick you out of your soul and heart, but instead, live your life without worrying about anything. Be careful to whom you give your power and energy, because in that way, you lose and you do not have access to yourself again. I know that you will say that it is easy for me to say that I am already there, but you are not, because I am a person who studies every day. I am closer to my heart, that is, I am already there. When you come there, you will see that the world is full of possibilities which you can use. You will need to roll up your sleeves and see what you really want in life, because everything that you wish for is possible and all you need to do is be unconditionally grateful and have no expectations. You can make exceptions that you are not like that, but you are forgetting that you can become like that and that your mind does not let you create the sea of possibilities. Let the Creator guide you towards your heart. Enjoy, forgive, love, sympathise, accept and learn from everything that is truly happening to you. The feeling will tell you everything. Thank you for reading.

Be the change you want to see in this world.

Let love and light shine on the Earth so that we can all find unity.

Ooops. I promised a happy ending.

"Believe in
yourself because
you are a divine
spark, shine and
illuminate your
way."

13.

Happy Ending

Well, here it is. Today, I live a comfortable life with my wife and son. 98% of the time we live suitably and in love. The other 2% are the times when our minds get in little arguments, but it is nothing like it used to be. Today, I am happy and free of the opinions of others. I live a humble and comfortable life together with my family. The most important things of all are health, love, peace, joy, compassion, acceptance and gratitude towards everything. For me, those are the real values and the highest achievements in life. That is why you should know that there is a possibility for you to achieve something like that in your life. Never give up because you should know that you are here to learn and to observe life, not to suffer. I love you and the light that is in your heart.

14.

Alternative Healings Therapies

What Is Ayahuasca?

I was in Colombia twice and I was present at plant medicine ceremonies with Ayahuasca. Ayahuasca is a brew made from two plants from the Amazonian rainforest. That amazing medicine is cooked for three days on a light fire and while it is cooking, shamans are singing, which gives the medicine a blessing. Ayahuasca has been used in the world for over 5,000 years, and it was made to clean our bodies, minds and souls.

In today's world, it is used a lot to help countless people who have different psychological or physical health problems. I was one of those people because of my depression when I had everything material, but I lost myself, and then I got the call from Ayahuasca. It might seem weird that you can get a calling for it, but from my insights, Ayahuasca is the soul of the Mother Earth. What she does after we take the medicine is that through certain visions and insights, we come to a connection with our heart. We come to a cleaner consciousness and a much more conscious life. Our actions towards the world around us change for the better and we live life more in love and with a truer connection with ourselves. Today, I am working with this wonderful medicine and I am trying to find ways to make the medicine available, because in the western world, it is forbidden by law. What I can say about that is that I have witnessed many wonderful positive transformations and a lot of people have stopped being addicted to strong drugs, alcohol and modern medicine, and they started living their lives from a new beginning. I would not like to get into the reasons why it is illegal, but it is up to you to question how is it possible and if you ever have a calling to go to a ceremony. This medicine is very recommendable, but you need to feel that within yourself, and you should find your way to go to a ceremony.

What Is Theta Healing?

If you go into Theta Healing, there you will find out a lot of things about your life and everything around you and how the Creator works. Theta Healing is a technique that guides us through meditation in Theta waves of the mind and the connection with our source or Creator Of All That Is. Theta Healing is an extremely broad technique that enters the pores of our lives, from our DNA to complete connection to the Creator. Of course, it goes to your relationships and love towards one another, and it is, in my opinion, one of the best courses. The Intuitive Anatomy is where you learn about organs and their purpose. After that course, I felt as if I had become a doctor. If you want to begin that technique, it is best that you do some of the lower courses first before this one so that you can master the technique. Anything that I find interesting, I learn fast, and I learnt a quite a lot in six months. I had six months of studying Theta Healing and I studied Intuitive Anatomy for around one month.

Theta Healing is a good technique, and it is very helpful but it can make people spin around in circles and in that way they are giving power to their subconscious mind.

15.

Message From The Creator

This Universe is a paradox. Everyone argues. You are looking for some fairness, but you do not live that kind of life. To live a life in justice, you need to live your life honestly and truthfully towards yourself and others. That is the only way you can change things. It is up to you to decide if you are going to accept that path, or if you are still going to execute your lies and false beliefs about how perfect you are and showing the world through social media that your world is beautiful when your face is full of make-up, masks and the truth is hidden underneath you. You look for an answer using drugs and alcohol. The solution lies within you, but you need to find the courage to go within yourself, and to face yourself and resolve the smallest detail of your reality. The best way is to really forgive. Not just to forgive and never forget. That is not forgiveness. Forgiveness is when you have the power to love someone who hurt you and to continue loving and accepting that person. If you do the opposite, you are just poisoning yourself from the inside and this leads to diseases and sicknesses. It is all inside of you and on you. The decision is yours. Your God loves you. Instead of putting each other down, love each other. You tend to be jealous and envious when someone has more than you, but everyone has as much as they believe they do. That makes you powerless and you lose your true essence and true power to create everything you ever wanted. You need to believe in Me, and you need to give control to just Me, and I will make sure that you have even more than your mind can imagine. That is all possible only if you find the true Me, and I Am here in you the entire time, but you escape from Me because you are afraid to see what I Am or what you are.

Do you call that life?

Life exists and does not exist. It is all true, it is all a lie, but the truth is Me who is in the centre of your heart, and I give you the impulse of life and I take care that your heart beats every day, if you live from love which is what I Am. I do not have the power to make your heart beat when you run away from each other and from yourself because it is hard for you to find Me. The devil as you believe does not exist, what does exist is your mind, which makes you do things, especially under the influence of drugs and alcohol, to serve the absence of the light which is inside of you. That is a trap I have shown you, because without it, the world would be too easy.

You should know that I find Myself and I find out new things about Myself every day. You just need to completely believe in yourself. That way you will find the truth, and your light, and love, which is unconditional inside of you and in Me. Be grateful to yourself and to Me for living every moment of this reality, because this reality is unique and you have a countless number of possibilities in you, and you need to remember these possibilities and find them. If you can afford to give yourself something you love, you are giving it to Me as a gift so that my love towards you is possible and I will give you true happiness. True happiness is not a current feeling. True happiness is everlasting. That is why often when you look for happiness, it is already there, without you needing to look for it.

You chose to suffer and act the victim because your mind was so hurt. Instead of leaving your mind to rest, you should submit to your heart and reside in Me. I love you all unconditionally, but you need to love yourself unconditionally because every part of your body, every atom of all of existence is perfect. It is just that your mind has invented the concept of personality and flaws in your appearance.

When you love yourself unconditionally, I love you unconditionally every day, but when you start to love yourself unconditionally, then humanity can be united in unconditional love. Do not look for answers in others because that way you give the power to others because the real power lies within you. Do not follow someone, follow yourself and your power, because that is how you get to know yourself and Me.

Your Creator

"Love and accept
yourself because
that way you will
love and accept the
Creator."

21 Recommendations For A Better Life.

1.   Bless every day because you have the power to do so.

2.   Send love to those who are taking you out of your heart. The ones who cast stones at you, you should cast bread at them.

3.   Love yourself the way that you would love the people around you.

4.   Accept responsibility for your life.

5.   Live life as if it is your last day alive.

6.   Forgive yourself and others for all the past moments.

7.   Living in the future makes you anxious.

8.   Live in the present.

9.   Accept yourself and accept everything that happens to you. There is a lesson behind every situation.

10. Let go of the role of victim from your life and be a hero. (Instead of pitying yourself, find an exit from the situation and act accordingly.)

11. Do not look for happiness, it is already here.

12. Believe in yourself and your personal power, which lives in your heart.

13. Do not procrastinate, start doing something.

14. You do not need to know the path, only the destination.

15. Do not judge others because you are judging yourself.

16. What you see in others is what you are.

17. Know what you want, everything is possible for yourself.

18. All energy put into something will eventually come back to you if it's unconditional.

19. To create, do things one by one with patience and gratitude.

20. Let go of the bonds and attachments on things and people. Live your life without attachments on things and people.

21. Be grateful for your life and everything that happens, no matter what.

Nino Appeared To Me At Mass.

It was an anniversary for my deceased brother Nino. It was on Christmas Eve of 1996. The priest started the mass, and everything was as usual. My mother cried because she remembered everything, and I could not help myself either. I cried every now and again when I would remember, or when the priest would mention Nino. Something interesting happened. As the mass went on, I moved to the present moment, although I did not know at the time that it existed. I simply stayed and I disconnected from the mass. There were children from Nino's class at the mass. They sat on the left side in front of me. In that moment, I could not believe what I saw. Nino was standing beside one boy who he was best friends with before he died. He did not look like a person though, that is, he did not have a physical shape. He looked like a light child. I knew that it was him and I started crying a lot. It lasted a few seconds and he disappeared. Later, I told my mother what happened. She did not believe me, and she thought that I was crazy. She sent me to a psychiatrist. When I was at the psychiatrist, I told him my story. He did not say anything or prescribe me anything. He said that I should come back in two weeks. Honestly, I was looking for help from someone who would understand me because that was real for me. I did not expect much from a psychiatrist. It was more like talk and then go home. I did not want to go to the second meeting. I saw that he could not help me. Thank God, I was younger, because if that happened when I was older, he would have sent me to an asylum. There was another time when I had a meeting with a psychiatrist. I was with my grandmother at a check-up in the same room. The doctor asked her if she could read thoughts. My grandmother said "no". At the time, I could. I started thinking that other people might be intuitive and that they could see the spiritual world, and that modern doctors would consider them to be crazy. I am not saying that that is the case with everyone, but what I deeply believe is that those people need understanding and not daily medicines (drugs), which take away their bodies and minds. They lose themselves to the point where they do not know what is happening to them.

Believe me, I had the chance to witness something like that after I had a road accident. I was taken to the hospital because I had a serious injury to my neck. I witnessed with full consciousness what tranquiliser pills do to people. After I took one, I felt like I was in a different space. Honestly, I would never take something like that ever again. I also saw how emotionless they treat people at the hospitals. There was a normal-looking young man in the bed beside mine. He looked out of the window and sadly said,

"I want to go home."

The nurse shouted at him and said,

"You aren't going anywhere, lie back down."

The man repeated himself twice, but the nurse kept repeating herself. In the end, they tied him to the bed and gave him some shot and then he fell asleep straight away. It was creepy to witness, and I had thoughts about me ending up like him going through my head. I can say that it looked like a scene from a horror movie to me. At the time, I did everything that they asked of me and, the next day, I lied that I felt better because I wanted to get out of there as soon as possible. My intention is not to attack modern medicine practices, my intention is to show you what happened in my life and what kinds of situations I have witnessed. To finish this off.

Today, I am certain that my brother did indeed appear to me. He wanted to show me that he was okay and that he still lives and that he is with me. I also know that he is with me every day, to be more exact, his energy of protection is with me. Yes, he was my protector even when we were little. He was smaller than me, but when I would end up in a situation where someone would attack me, he defended me, like David versus Goliath. He did this twice, where he attacked children twice his size to defend me. He was always there for me and he did not care about my jealousy. Unfortunately, I was not like that, but Nino was always a very calm person and he did not get into fights with people. I love you Nino and I will love you until I die.

In memorial on Nino Božić.

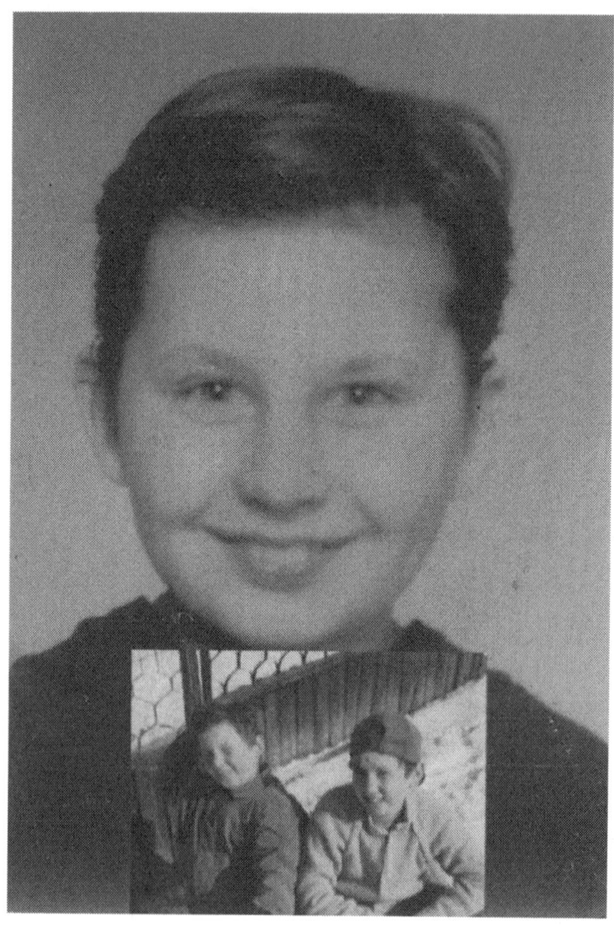

About the Author.

Alen is very passionate about shamanism and plant medicines, he has been doing spiritual work for the past 8 years. Alen has attended numerous spiritual ceremonies and workshops and is inspired by the likes of Vianna Stibal, Wayne Dyer, Neale Donald Walsch, Louise Hay, Eckhart Tolle, his spirit guides and the Creator. Alen lives and works in his native country, Croatia. Certain treatments that he provides are available online; but the plant medicine ceremonies are done in person. He also provides Theta Healing treatments. Ever since Alen had his spiritual awakening, his passion has been to empower people to find themselves and to achieve a better life through positive changes. He enjoys helping people find their personal power; never taking credit for the healing, because the healing is being done when a person is ready to help themselves. Of course, he is a good channel for helping such people. Alen believes in the personal freedom of the individual; and is ready to support anyone willing to find peace, love, joy, freedom and personal power. People either find Alen by word-of-mouth recommendations through his webpage secretofchange.org or his Facebook Page The Secret of Change.

About The Artist

Thank you to Danijela Cvitaš for her images on the back cover. She was born in 1979 in Zagreb, Croatia. Danijela finished degrees from the School of Applied Arts and Design and the Faculty of Textile Technology in the modern design department. She makes independent art exhibitions with the inspiration that comes from an inner awakening and recognition that she can let her being express itself freely through the expression of her heart and soul, and that it is possible to manifest what is invisible (from her inner world) to become visible. In that way, they unite physically and spiritually into a beautiful whole where life gets a magical and inspirational dimension.

Free Gift

Dear reader,

Thank you for taking the time to read my journey through change. After enjoying my book, I have a FREE gift for you on my web page secretofchange.org where you can sign up to receive a free meditation called "Cleansing with light", which I received from the Creator for you. This meditation can help you clean your energy with light on all levels but it all depends on your intention.

www.secretofchange.org

"The Secret

Of

Change

Is

YOU"

Made in the USA
Middletown, DE
01 February 2022